GROWING UP CHRISTIAN

GROWING UP CHRISTIAN

Why Young People Stay in Church,
Leave Church, and
(Sometimes) Come Back to Church

JOHN P. BOWEN

REGENT COLLEGE PUBLISHING
Vancouver, British Columbia

Regent College Publishing
5800 University Boulevard, Vancouver, BC V6T 2E4 Canada
Web: www.regentpublishing.com
E-mail: info@regentpublishing.com

Views expressed in works published by Regent College Publishing are those
of the author and do not necessarily represent the official position of Regent
College (www.regent-college.edu).

Unless otherwise indicated, Scripture quotes are from the New Revised
Standard Version Bible, copyright © 1989, Division of Christian Education
of the National Council of the Churches of Christ in the United States of
America. All rights reserved. Used by permission.

Library and Archives Canada Cataloguing in Publication Data

Bowen, John P
Growing up Christian : why young people stay in church, leave church, and
(sometimes) come back to church / John P. Bowen.

Includes bibliographical references.
ISBN 978-1-57383-431-5

1. Youth—Religious life. 2. Church work with youth. 3. Christian life.
I. Title.

BV4447.B69 2010   259'.2   C2008-906982-X

*This book is for four Leaders in Training from Pioneer Camp
who have a special place in my heart—*

Ben and Jen
Anna and Benjamin

CONTENTS

ACKNOWLEDGEMENTS

I suppose every book is really the product of a community, even when one person is named as "the author," and this one is no exception. In fact, the community aspect of this book's authorship will become obvious very quickly. So this is the time to say thank to the members of that community.

In chronological order, I need first to thank the family of Inter-Varsity Christian Fellowship. This organization nurtured me in faith from the time I was 15 and joined a high school Bible study group in my home town in North Wales. At university, they provided some of the best models of theological teaching and ministry one could ever hope for. And then, over twenty-six years on staff with IVCF, I was given great freedom to develop ministry skills and learn what I was gifted to do.

Most relevantly to this study, I want to thank that branch of the IVCF family called Ontario Pioneer Camps, where my wife Deborah and I had the privilege (and I do not use that word glibly) of serving with the Leader in Training program during the summers from 1981 till 1997. We met some marvellous people and learned some valuable lessons about God, life, and Christian ministry.

In particular, I want to thank the 1200 or so Leaders in Training who came through the program during those years, and very specially the 333 who took the trouble to fill out a copy of the questionnaire which forms the backbone of this book. All the responses were thoughtful, many were very poignant, and not a few were hilarious (intentionally so, I should add). My very sincere thanks to each one.

The late Jim Berney, then President of IVCF, and Peter Bloom, then Director of Ontario Pioneer Camps, gave me permission to use the camp's mailing list and to undertake this study. I am thankful to both of them, not just for that permission, but for their encouragement, and above all for their friendship.

These days, having finally left the staff of IVCF in 1999, I am a member of another extended community, that of Wycliffe College, an Anglican seminary at the University of Toronto. I want to say a warm thank you to them, especially to Principal George Sumner and to the Board of the College for the wonderful gift of a sabbatical during which I could work on this project.

Others have contributed to different aspects of this work. Four friends read the first draft and gave feedback that was incredibly detailed, honest and encouraging: Dr. Michael Knowles of McMaster Divinity College, Leanne Thorfinnson and Tony Lee, old friends from Pioneer Camp, and Dr. Graham Room of Bath University, UK. Dr. Andrew Irvine of Knox College, Toronto, and I talked about this project over great lunches at the Pheasant Plucker in Hamilton, and I am grateful for his good counsel and encouragement. James Penner, a colleague of Reginald Bibby at the University of Lethbridge, and Dr. Peter Brierley of Brierley Consultancy in the UK were generous and patient with their professional advice. Youth workers Valerie Michaelson, George Porter and Erin Biggs have given me good feedback from the front lines of youth ministry. And Bill and Gail Masson have given wonderful support and encouragement. Thank you, friends.

On the technical side, my sincere thanks to Myrna Talbot of the Talcon Corporation in Toronto for patiently teaching me how to use the data analysis software; to Mike Stiles, at Stiles Data Services, for his professionalism and thoroughness in the data analysis; to Lauren Matheson for his (in my opinion) genius in putting together the website where the surveys were posted; and, not least, to the Rev. Amy Bunce, my hard-working study assistant in the early days of the project.

My hope and prayer is that this book, the product of one extended Christian community, will serve to strengthen an even wider Christian community—the church across Canada—not least by helping us relate to young people. The best way we can do that, it seems to me, is by enabling the church to be all that the church has been called by its Founder to be. That's a challenge—but the only one a church should care about.

John Bowen
Wycliffe College, Toronto
Feast of the Epiphany, 2010

1

LIFE IS A HIGHWAY

The Who, the What and the Why of this Study

Where did we go wrong? That is the heartfelt cry of many Christian parents who see their young people drift away from the faith.

Consider the following scenario, and see if it sounds as familiar to you as it does to me.

Christine (not her real name) grew up in a strong Christian family, was a leader in her youth group, and sang in a music group which toured the province doing evangelistic meetings for other young people. Her parents thought maybe she would become a missionary, and prayed hard for her. Once she went off to university, however, something happened. She checked out one of the Christian fellowships, as her parents had encouraged her to do, but always seemed to have work to do on the night of the meetings. She got involved with a boyfriend who had no interest in faith, and in her vacations began refusing to go to church with the family.

The story of Christine could be multiplied a thousand times. If "life is a highway" (as the Canadian rock singer Tom Cochrane famously put it), some young people who profess faith in Christ never make it to their intended destination.

Christian parents find themselves wondering where they went wrong. Most parents' confidence in their parenting skills is fragile at the best of times. Under these circumstances, however, they quickly jump to the conclusion that their child's "loss of faith" means they must have failed.

If only they had been better role models, prayed more, had more frank discussions with their teenager, given stronger guidance about university, and a dozen other things, life would have worked out differently.

Worried and guilt-ridden parents are made to feel worse, of course, when they see their neighbour's child apparently doing well spiritually. Take Dave, for example. Dave was in the same music group as Christine, and went to the same university as her. Christine's parents had even hoped a relationship might develop between them because Dave was such a strong, stable Christian. He became a leader in the student fellowship and transformed it into a mature and thoughtful group. He is now engaged to another leader in the Christian fellowship, and he and Christine have lost contact. Dave's desire is to go on to seminary and become a pastor.

Sometimes Dave's parents and Christine's parents get together and talk about their kids. Dave's parents don't feel that they did anything different from Christine's in their parenting, neither is there any evidence that they were "better" Christians than Christine's parents. The two couples share their puzzlement, but the differences—and the pain—remain.

Of course, if you talk to Christine, you will get a different story. She would tell you about the time one of the spiritually respected leaders among the group came on to her during a church camping trip. (She was too embarrassed to tell her parents about that.) She would tell you about wrestling with difficult questions of faith, and how her parents and youth leaders basically shut her down, while her friends looked down on her for her "lack of faith." She would say that when she checked out the fellowship group at university, they seemed like a glorified youth group: she felt she had nothing in common with them. And when she met her boyfriend Robert, he respected her and listened to her in a way no-one else had ever done. She decided it was time to take a break from church, though she still felt a strong commitment to Jesus, and knew she might return to church one day.

What can parents, churches and youth workers can learn from the experience of Christian teens like Christine and Dave as they grow up and leave home? Is there anything which would help people like Christine be better prepared for the wider world and yet remain strong Christians?

RESEARCHING THE PROBLEM

For seventeen years, my wife and I worked in a Leadership Training Program at Ontario Pioneer Camp, a Christian camp in Ontario, Canada. Over that time, we worked with around a hundred young people aged sixteen and seventeen each year, making a total of over 1,200.

Naturally, we hoped that those who took the program would continue as Christians and as leaders in some way. In fact, I am in touch with many who have done just that—the Daves of this world. But over the years I have also come across many—like Christine–who for one reason or another have "dropped out" of Christian activity. For obvious reasons, I am not in touch with as many of these.

And, like Christine's and Dave's parents, I began to find myself wondering what had caused the difference. After all, we had all sung the same Christian songs, participated in lively Bible discussions, and (apparently) shared the same faith values.

So what had happened?

When people disappeared from the Christian scene, had we done something wrong? Did the church or their parents fail them? Did something in their life circumstances make it impossible to believe? Why did they give up on church? Why did some not want to be Christians any longer?

On the other hand, why did some carry on, grow in their faith, and become outstanding Christian leaders in different spheres, inside and outside the church? How was their experience different from those who were persisting and even thriving as Christians? What was going on?

Then I had the opportunity of a sabbatical from my teaching and decided to do some research to see what I could find out. Here is the question I decided to focus on: When a person was a promising Christian leader at the age of 16 or 17, what encouraged that person to stay within the Christian faith or to leave it?

This book is the result of that research.

I began the research with two hunches as to what I might find.

My main guess was that most of the factors influencing young people one way or the other would be to do with relationships. In particular, I assumed that friends and mentors would figure prominently.

My other hunch was that people would not have given up on faith because of intellectual problems. I did not expect a lot who had dropped out of faith to say things like, "I came to believe that the resurrection of Jesus was a hoax."[1]

For the most part, these hunches turned out to be correct, though, as is so often the case, the reality was far more complicated than I had expected.

WHO ARE THESE PEOPLE?

You need to know something about the people I was researching. There are three things they have in common:

---

1. One researcher who studied why Catholics leave their church agrees: "Theorizing about dropping out must start from the assumption that nonrational and interpersonal factors are predominant." Dean R. Hoge, "Why Catholics Drop Out," in David G. Bromley, ed. *Falling From the Faith: Causes and Consequences of Religious Apostasy* (Newbury Park: Sage Publications, 1988), 96.

1. An evangelical church background[2]

The majority of families who send their children to Pioneer Camp attend evangelical churches, particularly Baptist and Anglican churches (I will give some figures later), and their children have been brought up in that faith. Only a small proportion come from other traditions, such as Roman Catholic.

Some of the young people were not from homes that would consider themselves Christian of any kind, but became Christians through the influence of friends or church youth groups.

2. A Christian camp

You need to know something also about Pioneer Camp, because that is the "funnel" through which all these respondents passed at one point in their teens. Pioneer is owned and operated by Inter-Varsity Christian Fellowship, an interdenominational evangelical ministry to universities and high schools. The camp is spread over four sites and accommodates perhaps a thousand children between the ages of five and fifteen in the course of a summer.

As with many camps, a high proportion of the leaders have grown up through the camp system. The training program in which I was involved is a kind of four- or five-week bar- and bat-mitzvah, where those who had up to that point been served as children by the camp programs began to take on the adult responsibilities of serving the campers.

The leadership program itself is a healthy mixture of fun, work and study, geared both to the age-group and to the needs of the camp. The long-term effect of a camp and a program like this is

<hr>

2. The classic definition of evangelicalism is that of David Bebbington in *Evangelicalism in Modern Britain: A History from the 1730s to the 1980s* (London: Unwin Hyman, 1989). He says that evangelicals are those Christians who stress the importance of four things: conversion, activism, the Bible, and the cross.

difficult to measure, of course, especially as the participants get older and many other influences crowd in. (Some of those who were surveyed are now over forty.) In the chapters that follow, some talk about the influence of the camp on their spirituality, but most of what I discovered had to do with those other influences.

3. Middle class

Pioneer is not the most expensive of Christian camps, but it is certainly not in the "economy class" either. In the summer of 2010, one week at the camp cost $645 (Canadian); four weeks of the leadership training program cost $1,749 (Canadian). Thus most families who send their children there are generally middle class or upper middle class and can afford this kind of price.

4. A university education

Because of this background, it is not surprising that almost everybody from the program (98%) goes on to university or college. This is important to know, because the impact of university on a person's faith, for good or for ill, is far-reaching and long-lasting.[3]

The importance of these four things—church, camp, family income bracket and university—will become obvious as the story unfolds.

HOW DID THE RESEARCH HAPPEN?

With the help of the technical wizardry of Lauren Matheson (once in the leadership program himself), I prepared a questionnaire and

---

3. Other researchers have also noticed this: "Higher education tends to expand one's horizons and may also mean greater exposure to countercultural values. For many persons, such exposure has worked to erode traditional plausibility structures." C. Kirk Hadaway and Wade Clark Roof, "Apostasy in American Churches: Evidence from National Survey Data," in Bromley, 36.

Lauren posted it on a website. Then I contacted the alumni of the program by email or by letter.

The postal addresses were from the camp records going back to 1981, before the time of computers, so I was concerned that a large number would be out-of-date. However, to my delight, people began forwarding my email to one another, so that by the end, out of 1,258 possible respondents, I had email addresses for roughly 600. Partly as a result, the total of those who responded was 333, just over a quarter of those contacted.

Once they went to the website, respondents were invited to identify themselves in one of the following categories. For each group there was then a different questionnaire asking about their journey in faith—or away from faith (see Figure 1):

1. *"You still call yourself a Christian and are involved in church."* There were 251 who chose this survey, 75% of the respondents. I was fascinated to find that roughly one third of these (eighty-three), although they are active Christians today, had a time when they were away from church and/or faith.

Because the experience of these two groups is different, I will distinguish between them by calling them *Loyal Believers* (to indicate that they say they are still active in their faith, and have never been away from it) and *Returned Believers* (to indicate that they have had a time away from church and/or faith but have now returned).

2. *"You would no longer call yourself a Christian and have dropped out of church life."* There were fourteen who chose this survey, 4% of respondents. I will refer to these as *Former Believers*, to indicate that they say they have left Christian faith.[4]

---

4. This seemed better than the terms used by others who have researched this kind of question, such as "dropout" (C. Kirk Hadaway, *What can we do about Church Dropouts?* [Nashville: Abingdon, 1990]) or even "apostate" (Hadaway and Roof, in Bromley)! One respondent reacted to my use of (what I thought was) the milder term "dropped out" by saying, "I was a bit taken aback by the designation of this survey as being for Christians who have 'dropped out

3. *"You still consider yourself a Christian but have more or less dropped out of church."* There were fifty-seven who chose this survey, or 17% of respondents. I will refer to these as *Absent Believers*, to indicate that they say they have left church though not Christian faith.

4. *"You are still involved in church or other Christian activities but are no longer sure whether you should really call yourself a Christian."* There were nine who chose this survey, or 2% of respondents. Unfortunately, this is such a small number that little reference will be made to this category of *Uncertain Believers*.

5. There was also a space *for those who felt they did not fit any of the other categories.* This form of the survey had few questions, except for personal information, and people wrote in whatever they felt was appropriate. Four chose this option, or 1% of respondents. As it turns out, many of their stories are similar to those in the other categories, so I have included their comments in the categories they are closest to.

PROBLEMS WITH THIS KIND OF STUDY

There were three things which made this study difficult:

1. Trying to classify people is always tricky, especially when they only have five categories to choose from. Not surprisingly, the categories are not watertight, and a few people found it difficult to decide which to choose. One comments, "Even choosing which survey to answer gave me pause to think." Another, who finally decided to identify herself as a Former Believer, says, "I'd say that I was never really in [the faith] and I'm not all the way out the door now."

2. The exercise is also complicated by time. After all, the oldest people in the survey are in their mid-40s, are probably well

---

of church.' I have never thought of myself as a drop-out before!"

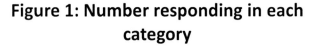

Figure 1: Number responding in each category

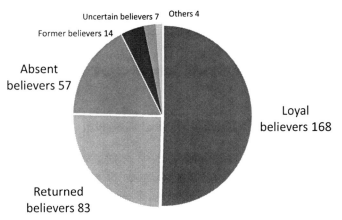

established in careers and (if they have children) parenting. The youngest, on the other hand, are approaching 30 years of age (or the equivalent). Biologically at least, the oldest respondents could be the parents of the youngest! This makes it difficult to draw conclusions across the years. For example, when someone of 38 self-identifies as an Absent Believer, it may not mean the same as when a 22-year-old says the same thing.

3. Any survey of this kind is only a snapshot in time. People are always changing. Some think that the most significant developments in faith do not happen until middle age or after, well outside the range of my respondents.[5] Obviously, the story is still

---

5. E.g. James W. Fowler, *Stages of Faith: the Psychology of Human Development and the Quest for Meaning* (San Francisco: Harper and Row, 1981).

being written. Some who have never moved away from church or faith will probably do so at some point. Researchers have discovered that some people do this more than once.[6]

At the same time, some who have moved away will undoubtedly return. One Absent Believer in her mid-30s actually states: "I am not currently involved in Christian activities; however, I am seeking a Christian community."

Inevitably, some people will have changed even since they filled out the survey.

FIRST IMPRESSIONS

As I read through the responses, there were a number of things that jumped out at me. I will offer a sampler of these here, just to whet your appetite, and then I will deal with each one at greater length in the following chapters.

(a) Loyal Believers were by far the largest group of respondents: 251 out of 333, or 75%. It was obvious from the beginning, of course, that Loyal Believers would be the majority of those who would reply to the survey. In any survey of "religion," it is the more "religious" who find it easiest to respond. [7]

Of course, that doesn't tell me anything about those who did not respond: one cannot argue from their silence. For all I know, every one of the 925 who did not respond may have become Zen

---

6. Peter Brierley has written that, in the UK and Australia, of those Christians who dropped out of church, 77% stayed away once, 19% twice, and 4% three or more times. (Personal correspondence.) The research behind these figures is described in Eddie Gibbs, *In Name Only: Tackling the Problem of Nominal Christianity* (Wheaton: Victor Books, 1994).

7. Other researchers have had the same experience, e.g. "Those who felt acceptably religious were more cooperative and forthcoming than those who were not self-assured in religious matters" (Dean R. Hoge, Benton Johnson and Donald A. Luidens, *Vanishing Boundaries: The Religion of Mainline Protestant Baby Boomers* [Louisville KY: Westminster/John Knox Press, 1994], 43).

Buddhists. What we can say, however, is that the overwhelming likelihood is that the proportion of Loyal Believers and Returned Believers among those who did not respond is far smaller than among those who did.

This response inevitably means that I will have more to say about the Loyal Believers than about the other groups. This does not mean that I think they are more important than the others, of course, simply that there is more I am able to say about them.

(b) I was in touch with several Former Believers in the course of conducting the survey. One emailed me early on and simply said, "Remove my name from your mailing list." (I did so). Another explained that she did not want to have to revisit questions which had been painful to work through some years ago. A third told a friend who invited him to participate, "Why would I care?" And I know of others who chose not to be involved. I have nothing but sympathy for such non-respondents—although I confess that I also feel some frustration because it would be very helpful to know something of their story.

This makes me particularly grateful to the fourteen Former Believers who did in fact take the time to fill out the survey. For them, it was probably a greater sacrifice than for those in the other groups.

(c) Respondents represent an amazing denominational diversity. In the space that asked about church affiliation, no less than twenty-nine denominations or traditions were given. (Some of these are the churches they grew up in, others are churches they belong to now.) By far the two largest denominations represented were Baptist (84 respondents) and Anglican (55). The full list is as follows (in alpha-betical order):

- Anglican Church of Canada
- Associated Gospel Church (AGC)
- Baptist (three kinds: Fellowship, Convention and North American Baptist)

- Brethren
- Brethren in Christ
- Christian and Missionary Alliance (CMA)
- Christian Reformed
- Church of Scotland
- Congregational (Four C's)
- Evangelical Free Church of America (EFC)
- Fellowship of Independent Evangelical Churches (FIEC: a British denomination)
- Free Methodist
- Lutheran
- Mennonite Brethren (MB)
- Non-denominational
- Orthodox
- Pentecostal
- Presbyterian (Presbyterian Church of Canada and Reformed Presbyterian)
- Quaker
- Roman Catholic
- Salvation Army
- Unitarian
- United Church of Canada (UCC)
- United Methodist
- Wesleyan, and
- Vineyard

Apart from Baptist and Anglican, the other groups with the largest representation were: Presbyterian (23), United (16), Christian and Missionary Alliance (14), Associated Gospel Church (11), and non-denominational (11). Some of the other groups only had one or two people mention them. (Figure 2 shows the proportions at the time when participants were at camp in their teens.[8]) We can

---

8. These numbers are unrepresentative of general denominational strength

Figure 2: Denominational affiliation as teenager

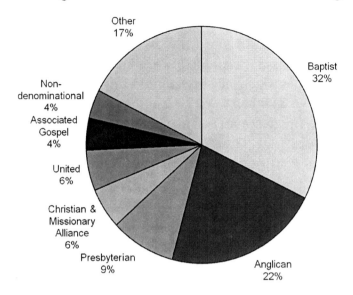

simplify the picture by saying that (apart from the "other" groups), 120 respondents were from conservative Protestant denominations and 94 from mainline churches.[9]

(d) Because Baptists and Anglicans are such large groups, from time to time I will compare their responses, because often they are very different from one another. Sometimes I think I know why the differences exist, but at other times I am simply observing the difference but cannot explain it. The question of how the spiritual

---

in Canada, where in 2001 Roman Catholics were 62%, United 14%, Anglican 10%, Baptists 4%, and other orthodox Protestant denominations around 5% in total.

9. By conservative, although it is not a very precise term, I mean such denominations as Baptist, Pentecostal, Associated Gospel Churches, Christian and Missionary Alliance, and Mennonite. By mainline, I mean Anglican, Lutheran, Orthodox, Presbyterian, Roman Catholic, and United.

formation of young people happens in different denominations would be a fascinating study in itself.

This question of denominations raises another point:

(e) It is remarkable how many people have changed denomination since the time they were teenagers. Three-quarters (249) have left the denomination in which they began life. Many would sympathize with the person who wrote, "I don't subscribe to denominations, but rather, prefer to find a specific church with a pastor and congregation that I relate to."

This research confirms what others have found, that changing denominations is a very common thing these days.[10] The most extreme example of switching I found comes from a respondent says, "I have changed from Christian Reformed to Baptist to Anglican to Christian Reformed to AGC."

At the same time, sociologist Reginald Bibby points out that the switching is often not as dramatic as it might sound, because it is often within church "families"—that is, from one conservative church to another, or from one mainline church to another.[11] The majority of changes among my respondents confirm this. Figure 3 shows how people have changed in their loyalty to church "family."[12] Sometimes, when the results are noticeably different among these four groups, I will comment on it.

In the chapters that follow, after each quotation I will give the category they chose ("Loyal Believer", etc.), their age at the time of the survey (if they did not indicate it, I will put XX), and

---

10. Donald C. Posterski and Irwin Barker, *Where's a Good Church? Canadians Respond from the Pulpit, Pew and Podium.* (Winfield BC: Wood Lake Books, 1993), 50.

11. Reginald W. Bibby, *Restless Churches: How Canada's Churches Can Contribute to the Emerging Religious Renaissance* (Kelowna, BC: Wood Lake Books and Toronto: Novalis, 2004), 34-37.

12. The total is only 249 because some did not belong to a church in their teens; Former Believers do not belong to a church now; and not all respondents indicate their affiliation now or then.

Figure 3: Numbers switching denominations

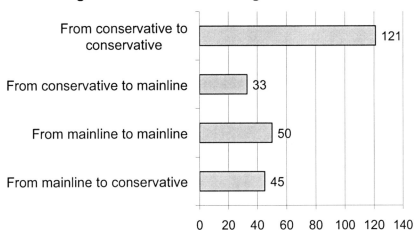

their denomination and whether they have changed it by saying something like "Anglican to Mennonite" (if they do not indicate a denomination, I will simply put XX.)

(f) Many of the respondents, whichever category they put themselves in, have experienced difficulties with church and with faith: many speak of finding "hypocrisy"[13] in the church, having values that differ from those of their church, encountering intellectual difficulties, and so on. If we add the four main categories together, no less than 25% of respondents report this as a problem. If we then remember that the proportion of those having problems with the church will certainly be higher among those who did not respond, the resulting total is staggering.[14] This theme of what we might call "the disappointing church" will be one I will frequently come back to.

---

13. I put quotation marks round this word because it seems to be shorthand for a wide range of experiences which will be illustrated in the chapters that follow.

14. I am grateful to James Penner for enabling me to make these connec-

(g) I did not ask those who say they are still Christians how they would currently express their faith. So I was startled to find that, in response after response, people spontaneously stated their faith in strong, personal and passionate ways. They testified to their love for God, their dependence on God, their gratitude to God, and so on. When I gave them a list of possible influences to choose from which would explain why they were still Christians, several of them criticized me because I didn't put "the grace of God" on the list![15] These are clearly people who are not involved in church and faith out of a grudging sense of obligation. They are involved because they feel strongly about these things.

(h) In different ways, the majority make a distinction between "personal faith" and "church involvement." These days, there seems to be a fresh realization across the Christian world that being a Christian is not a solitary adventure, with "church" as an optional extra. More and more people are talking about community as central to Christian faith. A number of respondents seem to be aware of this when they say things like, "I realize I need to get back to church" or "I know that Christianity is not a solitary faith."

Yet on the whole they still make a distinction between their faith and their belonging to a church. Many of them say something to the effect that, "It was my personal relationship with God that carried me through my time of disillusionment with the church." And in at least one case, the reverse is the case: a person continued with church, even though her heart was no longer in it: "I don't think I stopped going to church, but I stopped seeking God in my heart" (Loyal Believer 37, Anglican to Baptist).

This difference between "personal faith" and church involvement forms a consistent thread running through this research.

---

tions.

15. The trouble, of course, would be that if I had offered it as an option, no-one would want to discount it. It is far more interesting when people speak of it spontaneously.

(i) A lot of people say how difficult moving from one town to another has been for their church involvement. It is not easy uprooting from a faith community where you feel at home, comfortable and needed, to another where "none of the above" applies—at least, till you have been there some time. As Reginald Bibby says, "every time people move, about half of them will stop attending regularly."[16] Whether and why people resume church involvement is an issue I will explore. My conclusions are not as pessimistic as Bibby's.

Figure 4: Number of responses from each year

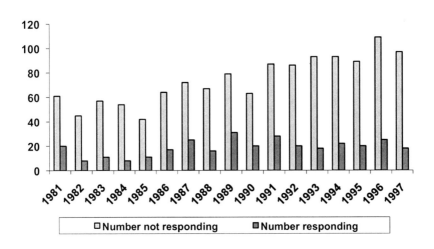

(j) I had thought that the number of people responding would be low from the early 1980s and higher as they approached the present. However, responses were scattered very erratically among the years. (See Figure 4.) The highest response was from 1990 (34.9%),

---

16. Reginald W. Bibby, *There's Got to be More! Connecting Churches and Canadians* (Winfield, BC: Wood Lake Books, 1995), 78. One third of church-leavers in the UK attributed their leaving in part to moving house. Leslie J. Francis and Philip Richter, *Gone for Good? Church-Leaving and Returning in the 21st Century* (Peterborough, UK: Epworth, 2008), 132.

and the lowest from 1984 (14.8%). The earliest year (1981) provided one of the highest response rates (32.7%) while the most recent year (1997) was one of the lowest (16.5%).[17] Partly because of this, I have not noticed any trends as one generation succeeds another.

A ROAD MAP

This chapter has been in some ways like looking at the map of a road trip we are going to make together. I have felt a bit like the navigator, pointing out some of the most prominent features we're going to pass along the way. Now it is time to get on board and start the journey and meet some of our fellow-travellers.

---

17. Eleven did not respond to the question of what year they were in the program.

2

FAITH FOR THE LONG HAUL

What Keeps Loyal Believers Going?

Anne grew up in a strongly Baptist home, but went to a lively Anglican church while at university. She was involved in a student fellowship at university, and during her summers went to work at the church camp she had attended as a child. She met her husband during the last summer there. Now she is married and involved in a Presbyterian church to which friends invited her. She has a group of women friends she meets with monthly over lunch, where they are quite vulnerable with one another about their spiritual lives. She struggles to have a personal devotional time each day but has more or less given up on that while her children are small. Her father died suddenly five years ago, and she had a hard time with that, not least since he had been significant in her spiritual formation. Her church was supportive through that period. She teaches Sunday School, and serves on the missions committee. Church politics get her down, and one previous pastor left after financial impropriety, but she hangs in with the church. She considers herself orthodox in terms of her theology, and some courses at a local seminary when she was first married helped deepen her faith. She finds herself more open-minded than she used to be on subjects like homosexuality, particularly since a good friend came out a few years back. These days she generally votes NDP, to her mother's surprise.[1]

Our culture assumes that young people will "give up" on church during their adolescence, and there is a feeling, often unspoken, that this is somehow normal and healthy. The language we use is revealing. The church, we are often told, is boring and rule-bound, formal and full of old people. Adolescents, on the other hand, need to experiment, spread their wings, kick over the traces, cut the apron strings, flex their cultural muscles, fly the coop, discover who they are. You've heard that kind of language: it represents a point of view that is popular and often unquestioned.

At least one sociologist shrugs his shoulders, seeming to feel that this is inevitable and perhaps even necessary: "The church can do little to change the nature of growing up in America."[2] Apparently, this is just the way things are, and ever shall be, world without end. When the church goes head to head with "the culture," the culture will always win.

What I discovered confirms that this pattern certainly does happen, but it does not apply to everyone. To my surprise, almost precisely half of those who filled out a questionnaire (168 out of 333) say they that they have never had a period of 6 months or more away from church and/or faith. This is a remarkable number.

Now, having said that, I need to repeat that these people are not a typical cross-section of Canadian young people: most of them grew up in evangelical homes where personal faith was taken very seriously. Nevertheless, since many of those who also had this kind of background either gave up faith altogether or turned away from it for a period, this is still a significant group.

Reginald Bibby makes a helpful observation:

---

1. The thumbnail sketches which open this and other chapters are not actual people, but are a composite representing the "typical" respondent in this category.

2. Hadaway, 92.

There is nothing written in the stars that requires young people to drop out during their late teen years. I suspect that most who say goodbye to the churches do so for one main reason: they don't find churches to be particularly enjoyable or gratifying environments.[3]

He is obviously right. Young people do not have to drop out of church. And when they do drop out, certainly one reason is that they don't enjoy church. However, there are several other reasons, and we will look at those in chapter 5 and 7. But first of all, I want to look more closely at these people who have never left either church or faith.

The first question I want to ask is: What on earth has kept these people in the faith? Our culture probably assumes there must be something peculiar and even unnatural about them. What is their problem? Are they in a state of arrested development? Do they simply not want to grow up and do what we all know is "normal"? Why haven't they done what young people are "supposed" to do? They clearly need to get a life!

There are many reasons they stay. The questionnaire asked them, "What would you say are the main factors that have enabled you to stay within the Christian faith?" These were the seventeen possible answers I offered them, plus a category where they could write in "Other" reasons I had not thought of:

- Having a church that was supportive and helpful
- Having models and mentors for me in my Christian life
- Finding helpful answers to the intellectual questions of Christianity
- My personal relationship with God
- Having friends who are Christians
- Finding help to resist lifestyle pressures in areas such as sexual behaviour or the use of alcohol

---

3. Bibby 1995, 75.

- Finding a life partner who shared my Christian commitment
- Christian faith helped me with the questions of everyday living
- Finding a different denomination or church from the one I was in as a teenager
- Wanting to follow the example of my parents
- My study of the Bible
- The LIT program at Pioneer
- Finding that the ethical views of the church coincided with my own e.g. on abortion, euthanasia and homosexuality
- I have children and wanted them to be Christians
- An ISCF, IVCF or other Christian community at school
- Christianity answers the big questions of life
- Staying involved with camp and/or camp friends after my LIT year

The results are shown in Figure 5.

To be honest, I had expected that "friends" would be the number one factor. More than one survey of young people has shown that the influence of friends is more important than any other.[4] I confess I was embarrassed not to have foreseen what their number one answer would be. I feel slightly better because everybody I have asked about this, including youth workers and parents, has also guessed wrong. The actual answer is:

MY RELATIONSHIP WITH GOD

The vast majority of Loyal Believers—89%—chose "my relationship with God" as "important" or "very important" to explain why they were still Christians and involved in church. Most of those who wrote in the "Other" space also took the opportunity to write about

---

4. The influence of friends has been a consistent finding in youth research at least from Don Posterski's *Friendship: A Window on Ministry to Youth* (Toronto: Project Teen Canada, 1985) to L. David Overholt and James Penner's *Soul Searching the Millennial Generation* (Toronto: Stoddart, 2002), 15–16.

Figure 5: Factors causing Loyal Believers to stay
(proportion indicating "Important" or "Very important")

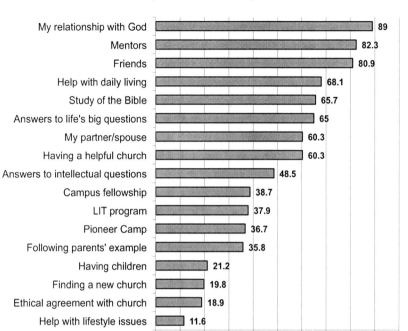

this relationship. These responses were from people of all ages and all denominations. The written comments on this subject are clear and passionate, and have the ring of authenticity. Many write about how their faith has brought them through testing times. Here are some of the things they write:

> No matter what circumstances I have experienced (especially in the last few years), nothing would make me run from God or turn my back on God. On the contrary, it is to God I run in times of trouble. (Loyal Believer 38, Baptist)

> During the separation period before my divorce, I seriously questioned my faith and what it meant to be a Christian. Do I turn my back on God or cling to him with all I've got? The answer, obviously, was to cling to God. After that decision, life

started to make sense again and I started making a new life which has turned out to be far better than before (kinda like Job's in a small way). (Loyal Believer 38, Baptist)

I have learned that only at the bottom of the deepest pit, when everything else is stripped away, when no one else has an answer or a book for me to read or a solution, only in the complete darkness and lack of direction do I hear God clearly and know that I am not alone. I found him cushioning the bottom of the darkest pit. (Loyal Believer 35, none to Free Evangelical)

The revelation of Christ's love and goodness is difficult to walk away from when it is a reality . . . Life would not make sense to me without the eternal perspective he offers. (Loyal Believer 23, non-denominational)

Others contrast their commitment to God with the failures of the church:

The church/God's people are broken but we must not let that brokenness interfere with our picture of a loving, righteous and faithful God. (Loyal Believer 27, Baptist)

I have never walked away from God because I have nothing without God. But, I have been VERY angry and even hated the 'Christian-ness' (perfection, pat-answers etc.) people portray! (Loyal Believer 27, Christian and Missionary Alliance to non-denominational)

If it hadn't been for my personal grip on God, I would have quit church in college, for good. (Loyal Believer 27, Anglican)

Some make a point of saying that, even though their relationship with God has been helped by church and friends, ultimately it doesn't depend on these human factors:

The biggest reason I'm still a Christian really has little to do with external things like church etc. I'm a Christian because every now and then I get a glimpse of the eternal: the Spirit moves in a person's life I'm close to, some passage of scripture reveals the eternal truth of God, or the Father speaks change into my life through prayer. (Loyal Believer 26, Anglican to Baptist)

Even if everything else was gone and every question in the world was posed, Christ would remain and that's enough for me! (Loyal Believer 22, Presbyterian to non-denominational)

Others make the point that the relationship does not depend on their own efforts to maintain it:

I know I have let God down many times. I have always known He will never let me down. (Loyal Believer 38, Baptist)

I see my faith powered by God, not myself or outside influences. (Loyal Believer 36, Christian Reformed)

I'm a Christian because I know that God is real—because I know him. That's the kind of truth that I could never really ditch, even if I wanted to. That's not to say I've always been super close to God. (Loyal Believer 25, Anglican)

Several say they have stuck with their faith in spite of difficulties. Others never seem to have thought about turning away, and nothing seems to have shaken their faith. It would be easy to respond by saying, "Aha, of course, a sheltered faith like that is not really worth much." However, we are not so quick to judge if someone says, "I have loved my country all of my life" or "I have always been close to my mother." The evidence is that a lifelong, strong faith can still be fully authentic. Here is one example:

I was raised in the faith, and I have always known and felt that there was One who was with me always, supporting and loving me—closer than a best friend, more secure than a parent, more loving than a spouse. (Loyal Believer 28, Anglican)

I suppose I should not have been surprised to find that the answer to the question, "Why do you still believe in God?" was "Because of

God!" One person spells it out: "Above all, I am a Christian because of my relationship with God."

Then, however, I find I want to probe a little deeper and ask, "So what exactly is it about your relationship with God that makes you stick with it?" Here are some of the themes that emerge in the answers people give:

- Life makes sense if God is there, when all else seems random: "Life would not make sense to me without the eternal perspective he offers."
- God is a refuge when circumstances are unbearable: "It is to God I run in times of difficulty."
- A damaged life can be put back together by God: "I started making a new life."
- God is an integration point for human beings: "I am nothing without God"
- God is a reliable companion: "I am not alone": God is "with me always."
- A sense of a dimension of reality which is inexplicable if there is no God: "glimpses of the eternal."

To me, these testimonies to the reality and power of "a relationship with God" are striking in both quantity and quality. This is thought-provoking for those involved in youth ministry. If a real and passionate relationship with God is what fuels long-term faith, it is worth asking how much of our program is devoted to helping young people develop that kind of relationship.

There are two ways people might criticize these responses, one from outside the church, the other from inside:

1. A cynic might respond by saying to those who believed through difficulties, "Well, if you can't handle your difficulties yourself, I guess you need to invent a God to help you out." But often the same cynic will say to those who have not faced major problems, "Of

course, it's easy for you to believe if you don't face the same difficulties that the rest of us experience in the real world."

We cannot have it both ways—on the one hand criticizing the faith of lifelong believers who have "led a sheltered existence" and on other hand belittling the faith of people who find God a source of strength in times of difficulty. I suspect the real problem for critics who want it both ways like this is actually faith itself, perhaps even the whole idea of God, and not believers.

2. Some Christians will say that the emphasis on "personal faith" which these stories uncover is unhelpful, since the point of Christian faith is not just that God wants to renew lots of individuals, but that God is bringing into existence a new community.

However, the New Testament seems to emphasise the importance of both individual faith and corporate faith. The apostle Paul, for example, says on the one hand that "Christ loved *the church* and gave himself up for *her*," yet at the same time, he is equally convinced that "the son of God . . . loved *me* and gave himself for *me*".[5]

The other thing to say is that the majority of respondents clearly show by their words and their actions that they do understand the importance of Christian community. One Loyal Believer speaks for many: "You can't be a lone ranger Christian." Many seem to have got the balance about right. Their personal faith has kept them going when the church let them down. Although it is less common for them to say so, I suspect the church has kept some going when their personal faith let them down.

One way this becomes obvious is that, after speaking of how important their relationship with God is, the influence of other people comes a strong second. For convenience, I am going to put

---

5. Ephesians 5:25, Galatians 2:20. Sociologists make the same observation: "Striking a balance between shared faith and individual freedom is necessary." Jackson W. Carroll and Wade Clark Roof, *Bridging Divided Worlds: Generational Cultures in Congregations* (San Francisco: Jossey Bass, 2002), 67.

together the effect of friends, mentors, partners/spouses, family, camp and church under the heading of:

THE CHRISTIAN COMMUNITY

Just over 60% of this group who have never left church or faith say that "having a church that was supportive and helpful" was important or very important in helping their faith continue. However, we might ask why that figure is not higher—would you not expect 100% of Christians to say church was "Important" or "Very important" to the maintenance of their faith?

What these responses make clear is that it is not just "church" in a formal sense—the community that gathers Sunday by Sunday—that encourages them. After all, "church" takes many forms, some of them very fluid. In a sense, something quintessentially "church" happens whenever Jesus' followers gather—whether for prayer or for social service, for a beer or for Bible study. Some of these informal, unstructured gatherings where Christians get together in groups large and small are described in what follows—and many rate higher than the 60% given to formal Sunday "church." This says to me that while it is good to encourage people to attend "church," it is needful at the same time for them to explore some of these other forms of Christian community, knowing that in the long run these will be necessary to sustain lasting faith.

Mentors

The human relationship that rates highest for helping people keep their faith is with a mentor. Just over four-fifths (82.3%) of Loyal Believers say this is "Important" or "Very important." What exactly is a mentor? My favourite definition is that mentors are those who "lead us along the journey of our lives. We trust them because they have been there before." They "fill a psychic space somewhere between lover and parent."[6] Ideas like leading, journeying, trust, love and parenting resonate deeply with Christian faith, and it is not surprising to find people referring to their mentors with great warmth:

> Mentors have been one of the strongest messengers of God's grace. . . I am grateful to them. (Loyal Believer 26, Anglican to Baptist)

> The Christian role models (mentors) I have had over the years have given me ambitions in particular aspects of my Christian walk, [and] this has been helpful—to have a particular person—when I was 'down' in my faith. For example, having a Christian role model (outside of family) when 'Why, God?' questions arose regarding family struggles. (Loyal Believer 24, United)

For some, the leadership program at camp was valuable because it offered just this kind of mentoring. One person has fond memories of the program for this reason, more than ten years afterwards:

> I loved the attention of the program, with adults being interested in who I was. That was good for me. (Loyal Believer 27, Baptist to non-denominational)

Normally, mentors come from outside a person's family. That is one reason they are so influential. Families are *supposed* to give us help and guidance: mentors on the other hand are volunteers. One respondent points out that mentors help with the transition from "family faith" to "personal faith":

> [Camp] plays the role of allowing kids to find themselves apart from their parents . . . and claim the faith as their own. They are more likely to do so if they encounter role models who are a few years older who are talented, intelligent, wise in the faith and inspiring people. (Loyal Believer 30, Presbyterian to Baptist)

---

6. Lawrence Daloz, *Effective Teaching and Mentoring* (San Francisco: Jossey-Bass Publishers, 1986), 17.

Of course, this does not always work out. Another respondent complains that at camp she was assigned a mentor who "knew my parents—which defeats the purpose entirely!" Thus it is interesting that one respondent in her 30s says her family had a mentoring role:

> Family have been my mentors and continue to encourage/ challenge my faith. (Loyal Believer 33, Baptist)

Some respondents do not single out the influence of mentors, but mentors get mentioned as one in a list of helpful influences:

> My personal time with God, Christian friends and older Christian mentors became very important to me. (Loyal Believer 26, Lutheran to Christian and Missionary Alliance)

> I think how I was raised, my own personal faith, mentors and friendships have helped with keeping my faith relevant. (Loyal Believer 25, Pentecostal to non-denominational)

> I think the keys are that mentors and communities that God placed me in were committed to holistic, intellectually honest faith—faith that lived with integrity. (Loyal Believer 28, Baptist to Free Evangelical)

I mentioned earlier that sometimes there are contrasts between Anglicans and Baptists in their responses, and here is the first of them. Baptists are far more likely than Anglicans to say that mentors were important to them: 84.4%. Anglicans, on the other hand, only rate the importance of mentors at 69.4%. I notice also that when those who began life in mainline denominations move over to conservative denominations, they also rate mentors highly, at 81%.[7]

Because these numbers took me by surprise, I do not have information to explain the difference, though I do have a hunch, and

---

7. In all these cases, these are the respondents who counted mentors as "Very important" or "Important."

it is this. Many mainline churches still exist with "Christendom" assumptions, harking back to a society where everybody was assumed to be a Christian, and it was not considered appropriate to talk about one's "personal faith." In evangelical churches, on the other hand, there is normally an assumption that people make a personal decision to be a Christian. This means that the choice of personal faith needs to be talked about, not least from the pulpit. Thus it becomes easier to talk about faith, and it is more natural to think of helping someone else in their faith. This shows up in the use of a word used in evangelical churches with a similar meaning to mentoring—"discipling"—where an older Christian helps a younger one to grow in faith. "Disciple" and "discipling" are not words much used in mainline churches.[8] The high rating that people give to mentors shows how serious it is if a church's ministries are lacking in this dimension.

Friends

A huge proportion of these Loyal Believers—80.9%—say that their friends are "Important" or "Very important" for their continuing in faith, with 18 adding written comments. The influence of friends on teenagers has been well documented, so there is no surprise here. However, these are not just friends with whom you might hang out on a Saturday night. The kind of friendships described here have a clear spiritual component:

> Whether it is in high school, university or in the working world, having a group of good Christian friends that will support and challenge me in my walk is the key principle, I think. You

---

8. Dr. Michael Knowles has pointed out in personal conversation that the tradition of Spiritual Direction bears a striking resemblance to the evangelical culture of mentoring or discipling. I will say something about this in Chapter 3. This whole area of how different denominations practice spiritual mentoring would be a very interesting one for someone to research.

can't be a lone ranger Christian. (Loyal Believer 29, Associated Gospel Church)

For me, the biggest factor which kept me walking with the Lord was the number of good Christian friends I had as a teenager. I met all of them through our youth program at church. (Loyal Believer 25, Mennonite)

What kept me going through the doubt and questions and pain of life was people who were there to stand beside me and cry with me and not judge my doubt and questions. (Loyal Believer 23, Anglican)

You can hear the spiritual note here quite clearly. These are friends who "support and challenge me in my walk" and who "stand beside me and cry with me." Others speak of friends who "helped me go deeper in my relationship with Jesus" and "push me to want more." One good thing about church youth groups is that young people make friends who believe as they do. However, these friendships alone are not likely to influence faith in the long term unless they have this self-motivated spiritual dimension, where the joys and struggles of faith can be openly shared. This requires a level of trust where friends can ask each other personal questions such as, "How are you doing in your faith?" "Can I pray for you?" "Can I tell you how God is working in my life?" without being considered rude or inappropriate.[9]

As with the topic of mentors, on this topic of spiritual friendship there are some big differences, depending on people's denominational background, and the simple statement that 80.9% value their Christian friends actually masks some deep distinctions. What I noticed is that those who have always been in conservative churches

---

9. Dean Hoge defines a plausibility structure as: "networks of persons in constant contact who hold to a common worldview and set of moral commitments." That appears to be the same thing as my respondents are describing. Hoge, Johnson and Luidens,165.

are far more likely to put a high value on this kind of "soul friendship" than those who have always been in mainline churches: 88% in conservative churches over against 62% in mainline churches.

What is going on there? Once again, I can only guess, but my experience suggests that in mainline churches it is not quite polite to talk openly about one's personal spirituality. Friendships can be strong and candid, of course, with conversations ranging freely from politics to sexuality. Nevertheless, for many in mainline churches, an individual's faith and feelings about faith are off limits. They are simply between the person and God. But the presence or absence of this kind of friendship is a major factor in people's continuing in faith.

Unfortunately, not every youth group or university fellowship fosters such depth of relationship. The question is: How can churches and youth leaders, whatever their denomination, encourage that kind of "soul friendship"? Indeed, how many churches model that kind of friendship even among their adult members? It would be interesting to discover where it was that respondents found that deep spiritual kinship. Some mention camp, or a youth group, or a campus fellowship, informal contexts where such intimacy is more likely to occur (maybe one reason wise churches encourage such activities). It is possible that some found this kind of relationship in churches, but if so they do not mention it.

Marriage

Marriage, of course, is another form of (very small!) Christian community, and 60.3% of all Loyal Believers say that their spouse was "Very important" or "Important" in nurturing their faith.[10] The proportion of these Loyal Believers who are married is 58.8%, so

---

10. Again, there are some significant variations: Anglicans rate the value of marriage to their continuing in faith at 54.2%. Those who have remained in conservative traditions rate it at 66.3%, and those who have moved from a mainline to a conservative church at 71.5%.

there is almost a 100% affirmation of marriage as a faith-enhancing factor. One says simply, "I married a Christian whose faith reflects mine." (Loyal Believer 38, Presbyterian) Another says, "Praying and reading with my husband has been a wonderfully nurturing activity both for our spiritual lives and for our marriage." (Loyal Believer 23, Presbyterian to non-denominational)

For some, marriage occurs as one item in a list of positive influences:

> Getting married to John, finding a church that was Christ-centered, and then having children and wanting them to first know the Lord in an everyday way, has all contributed to my commitment to our church. (Loyal Believer 38, Presbyterian to Baptist)

> For me, although church and my own faith were important, the biggest contribution to my ongoing commitment to Christianity is having friends, family and a spouse who share my beliefs to a smaller or greater degree such that we have at least a common starting point for making decisions, having discussions, etc. (Loyal Believer 34, Baptist to Anglican)

Campus fellowship

University is a crucial time in many people's development, socially, intellectually, and not least spiritually. For this reason, denominations have often founded chaplaincies to help their student members work out an adult faith. Interdenominational campus ministries such as Inter-Varsity Christian Fellowship, Campus Crusade for Christ and Navigators began as means of evangelism in universities, but, over the years, have also become a place where students from Christian homes have tried to work out their questions of faith. How have such groups affected those who responded to this survey?[11]

---

11. I wonder whether perseverance in faith is easier for those who have been involved in an interdenominational group, rather than a denominational one. For

Of Loyal Believers, 38.7% say that campus fellowships were "Important" or "Very Important" to them in maintaining their faith. The number is virtually identical for Returned Believers. One speaks of such a fellowship having "a HUGE impact on my faith."

Of all Loyal Believers, however, those who grew up in mainline churches were more likely to find such groups helpful. For example, those who have always been in mainline churches rate campus groups at 44.5%, those who have always been in conservative churches at 33.6%. This may be in part because many conservative churches offer their own "College and Career" groups which function as alternatives to fellowships on campus.

Since Pioneer Camp is part of the parent organization of Inter-Varsity Christian Fellowship[12], it is not surprising that 72 name IVCF as the student fellowship they were involved in. Another nine were involved in Navigators and seven in Campus Crusade.

So how exactly did this involvement help people in their faith? There were fifteen written comments, including these:

- A community where we could learn and grow together
- An outlet for further growth in my faith
- Instrumental in strengthening my faith and making it real
- Helped me greatly keep a focus on my Christian worldview
- Fundamental to shaping my faith and who I am now

Some say how important it was for them to find role models among people in their own age group:

I was awed by the spiritual maturity of some of the people in IVCF. (Loyal Believer 31, Anglican to Free Methodist)

---

one thing, it would make the denominational switching that is so common—and helpful for many—an easier thing to do. This is a subject for further research.

12. A number of campus staff work at camp in the summer, as I myself did for many years.

For others, a university fellowship was the chance to be treated as a gifted and competent adult away from the church community from which they came:

> My IVCF university group gave me freedom, respect, an opportunity to serve and use my gifts, and love. (Loyal Believer 30, Brethren to Anglican)

Some say straightforwardly that the fellowship was a safe place to explore faith and ask the questions that could not always be asked at home. Words like "question," "challenge," "seek" and "honest" crop up often:

> IVCF while I was an undergrad was a great support to me. It provided a place for me to question and challenge my faith, to establish community and find housemates, to hone my talents and abilities. (Loyal Believer 29, Baptist to Anglican)

> Helped me to challenge assumptions in faith and truly engage the world. (Loyal Believer 25, XX)

> IVCF was essential for me. I would not be a salty Christian if it were not for that interactive, seeking, inclusive, honest environment. (Loyal Believer 24, Anglican to non-denominational)

A campus fellowship is also one of the places friends are made, and often those friendships are of the spiritual and long-lasting kind that shows up as a long-term influence on people's faith:

> I made a lot of life long friends, including my husband, and it is these relationships that have continued to challenge me and push me to want more. (Loyal Believer 27, Christian and Missionary Alliance to non-denominational)

This is not to say that people's experience of campus fellowships was invariably good. There were clearly some groups that were not open, questioning and encouraging, and did not give the kind of help that might have been expected. Those stories will be told later.

But on the whole, for most Loyal Believers at least, campus fellowships did help them make their faith their own and to grow into Christian adults.

Camp

The purpose of this research was never simply to find out the long-term impact of Pioneer Camp. Nevertheless, the responses I received contain many references to camp—both positive and negative. In terms of why people keep going in their faith, camp is obviously one of those influences which help. I know that similar things could be said of many Christian camps which help young people at a crucial time in their faith. Pioneer is probably typical of Christian camps, in both the good and the bad they do.

Just over one-third—36.7%—of Loyal Believers mention the long-term influence of camp, often saying things like:

> It was there I first made a commitment to God. It was there that
> I first experienced God's presence in worship. It was there that
> I was inspired to take ownership of my spiritual journey. It was
> there that I was inspired by the breathtaking lives of certain
> highly committed Christians. (Loyal Believer 33, Presbyterian
> to Methodist)

Roughly the same number mention the leadership training program specifically, although for many it was a long time ago.[13] This Returned Believer speaks for many Loyal and Returned Believers:

> My Leader-in-Training year really doesn't impact my staying a
> Christian now—but it was a huge spiritual growth time at that

---

13. Anglicans rate the influence of camp in general at 33.3%, Baptists at 48.4%. With the leadership program, however, the ratings are reversed: 37.5% of Anglicans rate the program as important, compared with only 25% of Baptists. Perhaps the close fellowship and intensive learning experienced in the leadership program is less common for Anglican young people.

stage in my life and at that time allowed me to stay within the Christian faith.[14] (Returned Believer 38, Christian Reformed)

A dozen Loyal Believers write additional comments about camp, particularly as a place they found a supportive Christian community:

> The biggest spiritual impact on my life as a maturing teen/ young adult was definitely spending 10 summers working at Pioneer. I would not be the person I am today if it was not for camp. (Loyal Believer 34, Anglican to Mennonite)

> [I was helped by] My deeper . . . friendships formed while working in the camp over a number of years. (Loyal Believer 33, Associated Gospel Church to Anglican)

> The help of Christian friends, particularly those from Pioneer, has helped me live in God. (Loyal Believer 28, Anglican)

The words "friends" or "friendship" come up in the majority of these comments. C. S. Lewis once said that "Friends [are normally] side by side, absorbed in some common interest" and that "Friendship must be about something."[15] A Christian summer camp, where leaders are charged with the care and welfare of children, where they plan and lead fun events, and where they support and pray for one another, provides a powerful matrix for that kind of friendship to develop. We have already seen how important those friendships are for maintaining faith. Thus one of the long-term benefits comes only to those who return to the camp year after year and build the friendships that then become a mainstay of lasting faith.

Family

---

14. It would be a very worthwhile research project to consider the long-term impact of short intensive youth programs like this, whether interdenominational (like Pioneer Camp) or denominational.

15. C. S. Lewis *The Four Loves* (London: Collins Fount Paperbacks, 1960, 1977), 58–59.

The vast majority of respondents are from Christian homes, so at first sight it is rather surprising that only one-third (35.8%) say that their parents were a major influence in their "keeping the faith."[16] However, 24 Loyal Believers write in comments about the importance of family for faith (compared with 18 who write about their friends).

> The fundamental factors that have influenced me keeping my faith were my parents and their example of consistent Christian lives. (Loyal Believer 38, Baptist)

> I really believe that my continued Christian faith is a legacy of my upbringing, and the excellent and matter-of-fact way that Christianity was presented in my early life. It just always was there, from my home life, to my camp life (over 13 years of Pioneer). (Loyal Believer 36, United to Anglican)

> I think in my life overall, my parents were the biggest influence and contributors to my faith—helping me to get a good foundation on which to build. (Loyal Believer 34, Baptist to Anglican)

> I believe strongly that the prayers of my parents and therefore God played the most important role in my faith continuing. (Loyal Believer 33, Associated Gospel Church to Anglican)

> I believe that, first and foremost, the vibrant faith of my parents has spurred me on to continually embrace my faith. (Loyal Believer 30, Presbyterian to Anglican)

> My father's role (and then others) who believe that God is real AND ALSO LIVE their lives as if this is a reality. This has opened me to the presence and reality of God. (Loyal Believer 29, Anglican to non-denominational)

It is not only parents who receive credit here, however: siblings and grandparents are also singled out for their prayerfulness and

---

16. Again, there seems to be a difference according to tradition. Most of the groups rate the importance of parents at around 30%. However, for those who have gone from a conservative church to a mainline church, the figure is 42.5%.

modeling of what an active Christian life can look like. There is no guarantee, of course, that faithful parents will produce faithful children. Other chapters will describe the pain, often accompanied by anger and guilt, that is produced on both sides when children reject the faith of their parents. However, contrary to popular mythology, many children do continue in their parents' faith, and, when they do so, they seem very glad to give credit to their family.

A third category of influences concerns what I will call practical factors—help with daily living, study of the Bible, ethical concerns, lifestyle pressures, and finding answers to spiritual questions.

PRACTICAL FACTORS

For some reason, although significant numbers choose these options from the list offered, few choose to offer written comments on these topics. For example, though 65.7% indicate that "My study of the Bible" was important or very important to them, there are no written responses on the topic. Here are some of the responses I did receive:

- Help for daily living (which 68.1% said was "important" or "very important"): Christianity helpful in my work. Decision making, social justice issues, etc. (Loyal Believer 37, Baptist to Anglican)

- Finding answers to life's big questions (65%)[17]: "I think the biggest thing for me is that Christianity has helped me make sense out of a lot of life's hurts and confusions. I guess everybody is looking for an answer to those kinds of things, and I have found my answer in Christianity." (Loyal Believer 23, Pentecostal)

---

17. This is a more important consideration for those who have gone from mainline to conservative—72.8%; for those moving from conservative to mainline it only rates 51.5%. Why there should be this disparity is intriguing: a subject for further research.

- Finding helpful answers to the intellectual questions of Christianity (48.5%)[18]: "The intellectual plausibility of Christianity. I don't think you can 'prove' Christianity to anyone. I do think you can show that it is just as plausible though" (Loyal Believer 29, Anglican to non-denominational); "This is absolutely critical for me. I examine and ask questions regarding calculus and chemistry, and I would have to be insane to not ask equally tough questions regarding my faith. (Loyal Believer 24, United)

Lifestyle Pressures

Although I said that there are not many write-in comments under this heading of practical factors, there is one exception, and that is in the area of "lifestyle pressures." Although only 11.6% say that "Finding help in resisting lifestyle pressures in areas such as sex and drug and alcohol abuse" was "Important" or "Very Important,"[19] when asked to specify what those pressures were, sixteen chose to write comments.

One reason I asked this question was that many youth ministries take a lot of time and trouble to help young people with what society considers "the big issues" for youth—drugs, alcohol, and sex. I was interested to know whether young people felt that the church's efforts in those areas actually worked.

The fact that only 11.6% identified this as "important" or "very important" makes me wonder whether churches perhaps put too much emphasis on this area—not that it should be ignored, of course, but perhaps made less central. Thus, of those who chose this option, only four write that drugs, alcohol or sex were areas

---

18. The people for whom this is least important are those who have always been in conservative churches—44.1%; it has been most significant for those who have moved from conservative to mainline churches—63.7%.

19. Among Baptists, 20% say this is important; among Anglicans 12.5%.

where the church's support helped them maintain their faith.[20] One Returned Believer actually comments that in her experience youth ministry:

> Focused far too heavily on sexual pressures, drugs and alcohol, and for me those were not strong pressures at all. It was the introduction to other religious traditions, other students' doubts, other lifestyle choices in general that hit me broadside. (Returned Believer 36, Baptist)

Having said that, some comments on these issues are particularly poignant, such as this:

> The area that I struggle with is on the sexual side of things. I have had a problem with pornography, but have surrounded myself with people to keep me accountable and pray with me. (Loyal Believer 30, XX)

Two others, however, indicate ethical areas unrelated to drugs, alcohol or sex. They found support in their faith over issues like:

> The drive for success and monetary assets—car, house, clothes etc. (Loyal Believer 32, Presbyterian)

> Stress management (worry), materialism, gossip, self centered-ness. (Loyal Believer 31, Baptist)

Two comments indicate concerns over sexual issues combined with concerns over other lifestyle issues:

> Honesty; sexual pressures; desire for more; hurried lifestyle. (Loyal Believer 30, Christian and Missionary Alliance to Baptist)

---

20. Reginald Bibby agrees. In the final chapter of *Canada's Teens: Today, Yesterday and Tomorrow* (Toronto: Stoddart, 2001), he has a series of questions and answers. He writes, "Q: Are we fussing about some things we shouldn't be fussing about? A: Yes. Drugs and sex, for starters"(317). (His response is actually more nuanced than this startling exchange might imply.)

Sexual behaviour, looking negatively at society's less fortunate, abusive alcohol and drug consumption. (Loyal Believer 29, Baptist)

Another points out that the most troublesome issues actually change over time:

Before marriage: premarital sex temptations. Now: materialism. (Loyal Believer 29, Baptist)

One sad response suggests that whatever teaching is given about sex and alcohol, for some it will be ineffective anyway:

I actually haven't found help to resist the pressures because my life has actually become quite divided since I entered the working world. To be quite honest, I have succumbed to the pressures of drinking alcohol (sometimes to excess) and to having sex outside of marriage. (Loyal Believer 29, Baptist to Anglican)

If there is a lesson to be learned here, it seems to be that while it is important to teach young people about the traditional problem topics, it is important not to give the impression that these are the only lifestyle issues Christians should be concerned with. Christianity also has important things to say about topics like materialism, gossip, honesty[21], and the pace of life. Thus youth groups which offer young people broad and holistic teaching about "lifestyle issues" are laying strong foundations for the future as well as the present.

MULTIPLE FACTORS

Not surprisingly, nobody credits a single source for their ongoing spiritual life. As in the examples I gave above, many respondents list two, three, four or more influences. As one person comments,

---

21. A 2000 study of US high schoolers found that 80% had cheated in school; 53% of those felt it was "no big deal." Cited in Bibby, *Canada's Teens*, 18.

"I don't really think there is a single motivation keeping me 'Christian'." Another writes: "Almost every category listed has some effect on an individual personality." Others say:

> God used a variety of people, circumstances, his word, my family and many, many other things to help develop and strengthen my faith. There is no one particular thing that is responsible for my faith today except for the grace of God and his interaction in my life. (Loyal Believer 38, Baptist)

> I think the keys are that mentors and communities that God placed me in were committed to holistic, intellectually honest faith—faith that lived with integrity. My parents, camp, my childhood church, Trinity Western University, my current church, home groups, and my work environment now [at a Christian school] all contributed to the full development of confidence in a sovereign, loving God. (Loyal Believer 28, Baptist to Free Evangelical)

> The church I went to at university provided for spiritual care and the use of my gifts. Thus, my personal time with God, Christian friends and older Christian mentors became very important to me. (Loyal Believer 26, Lutheran to Christian and Missionary Alliance)

Churches which want to strengthen the faith of their young people need to bear this diversity in mind and not rely too much on any single source of nurture.

This chapter has looked at why Loyal Believers have stayed in church and in faith, in spite of all the cultural pressures to the contrary. So does this mean believing has been easy for them? What has happened to their faith over the years? And what exactly do they do with their faith? The next chapter will look in greater depth at the lives of this group.

3

STAYING ON TRACK

Loyal Believers Struggling to Grow

What more can be said about these young people who have done this counter-cultural, counter-intuitive thing of staying with their religion? We need to get to know them better, to figure out what it is that makes them tick and what they look like.

One thing that stands out sharply from the data is that these people have not stayed in church because they have found it an easy option. Many of them have had huge challenges, especially in their experiences of suffering. Their faith has also had to find ways of dealing with a wide range of pressures both intellectual and cultural.

Through all this (and often *because* of all this), these people have grown in their faith. They have not been intellectually or spiritually static. They have had no interest in occupying "the comfortable pew" as passive spectators week by week. The image of working out comes to my mind. These people have exercised the muscles of faith, and their faith has grown strong and resilient as a result. Not surprisingly, most have been active leaders in their congregations.

Let me start by passing on to you some of the difficulties these respondents describe, and you will see how they have responded

CHALLENGES TO FAITH

These 168 respondents were given the question: "What, if anything, has most caused you to consider giving up the Christian faith over the years?" The options I offered them were these:

a) The influence of peers who did not believe as I did
b) Lifestyle choices on my part which were different from the expectations of the Christian community in areas such as alcohol abuse
c) Hypocrisy among Christians
d) Having too many difficult unanswered questions about the Christian faith
e) A catastrophe (e.g. incurable disease, accidental death) among those close to me
f) Dating someone who was not a Christian
g) Feeling that I could no longer accept the exclusive claims of Christianity
h) The need to be different from my parents
i) Feeling that God had let me down (e.g. unanswered prayers)
j) Moving away from significant Christian community
k) Feeling that I was being judged by the church
l) Church seemed irrelevant to the questions of everyday life
m) Disagreeing with various ethical beliefs in the church, e.g. abortion, euthanasia, homosexuality
n) Feeling that my relationship with God was not real
o) Feeling overwhelmed by the expectations of church involvement

The results are in Figure 6.

This question was another which showed up some striking denominational differences. Those who had never thought about giving up their faith included 74.2% of those who had always been in conservative churches and 65.3% always in mainline churches. The figures for those who have switched traditions are much lower:

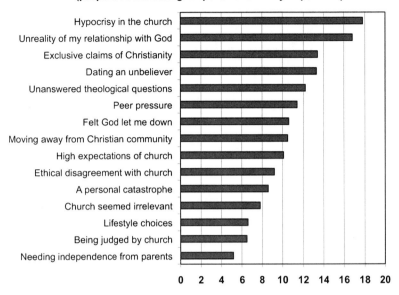

What challenged the faith of Loyal Believers?
(proportion indicating "Important" or "Very important")

54% of those who switched from mainline to conservative and only 44% of those who switched from conservative to mainline. (See Figure 7.)

I can only speculate about why these differences might exist. Maybe there is a natural conservatism among those who do not switch traditions which would make it less likely that they would consider giving up their faith under any circumstances. The higher number in conservative churches may be simply that personal commitment is emphasized more in those churches. Mainline churches, on the other hand, often do not maintain membership lists or require members to sign a statement of belief.

The figures for those switching traditions are intriguing too. I would like to know how often the switch was connected with the crisis of faith. Were those who moved to a more conservative church looking for a stronger foundation for their faith? On the other hand,

Figure 7: Who considered giving up faith?
Percentages of Loyal Believers

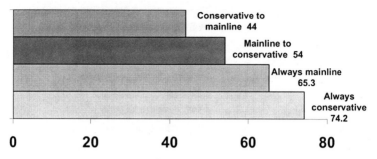

were those who switched to a mainline church looking for a church where less certainty about faith was more acceptable?

When I posed the same question about challenges to Returned Believers, their answers were different, and I will talk about them in a later chapter. But it is obvious that even those who have not been "away" have had significant challenges.

Some of them seem to belong together:

- Some are challenges on the intellectual level: "the exclusive claims of Christianity"; "too many difficult unanswered questions";
- Others might be called lifestyle challenges: "dating an unbeliever"; "peer pressure"; "ethical disagreements with church"; "lifestyle choices";
- Some were disturbed to find "many Christians to be mean, bitchy and hypocritical, while many non-Christians were friendly, kind and respectful" (Loyal Believer 26, Anglican);
- Yet others are challenges in people's relationship with God: "feeling that my relationship with God was not real"; "feeling that God had let me down."

None of these, however, was strong enough to destroy their faith. The factors described in the last chapter—their relationship with

God, mentors, friends, and so on—obviously enabled them to deal with the stress.

The two biggest challenges for these people, however, have been (a) the church and (b) suffering, so I want to say something more about these.

(a) Problems with the church

Many of the stress points in these people's faith journey have been to do with the church. Here are some of the things they say have been "Important" or "Very Important" challenges:

- hypocrisy in the church 17.8%
- lack of community 10.5%
- high expectations laid on them by the church 10.1%
- ethical disagreement with church 9.2%
- the fact that "church seemed irrelevant" 7.8%; and
- being judged 6.5%.[1]

This is a long list of problems. Remember too that these are the Loyal Believers, people who have never been away from church. These are not disillusioned members who have left in disgust. If they were, we might be able to find ways to explain away these criticisms. No: these are the frank observations of the church's friends. They deserve to be heard and taken seriously.

Here is a particularly striking example:

---

1. Baptists and Anglicans experience these problems differently. Anglicans are more likely to be challenged by hypocrisy (33.4% compared with 20% among Baptists), lack of community (20.9% compared with 13.3%), high expectations of church (17.4% compared with 7.4%), and the irrelevance of church (16.7% compared with 10%). Baptists, however, are more likely to have felt judged by the church (16.7% compared with 4.2% among Anglicans).

I found many so-called good-Christians to be very cliquey
and unfriendly to 'outsiders'. One of the biggest bitches I have
ever met, looked good as a [Christian camp] counselor, but
was nasty when she thought no one was looking . . . When
I started college, I found many non-Christians I met to be
great, accepting, loving people. Heck, the non-Christian guys
I dated in college were totally respectful of the fact I wouldn't
sleep with them, while many Christians I went out with (even
prominent church types) were so eager to screw me, it was
embarrassing! I would turn down a nice considerate respectful non-Christian guy, only to accept the date of a missionary/
church leader type guy, and find out he'd had a lot of sexual
partners and was eager for one more! And lying to church leadership about it too! (Loyal Believer 27, Anglican)

Because all the groups who responded had criticisms of the
church, I will wait till we have heard from all them before putting
the positive side: what it is they hope to find in a church. That will
be in chapter 9.

Even though "hypocrisy in the church" ranks as the number one
challenge to people's faith, the one they tell most stories about is the
one that came in at number eleven: suffering. One respondent calls
this issue "The Big One."

(b) Suffering

Only 8.6% in this group who have never been away indicate strong
agreement that "a catastrophe" challenged their faith. (The number
was somewhat higher—12.5%—among Returned Believers.) Yet
22 people in this group write about how suffering has challenged
their belief in a loving God. In fact, more people in this group say
something about suffering than in any other group. The stories are
powerful and poignant. What are they about?

Many speak of an untimely death, particularly that of a parent:

My father was killed in a motor vehicle accident when I was 19
years old. (Loyal Believer 34, Presbyterian)

When I was 10 my father was killed in a motorcycle accident. At 15, my mother died from multiple myeloma. (Loyal Believer 33, Baptist)

The death of both my parents through cancer was very difficult to endure. (Loyal Believer 32, Baptist to Anglican)

Why do bad things happen to good people? A person I knew was murdered. (Loyal Believer 30, Christian and Missionary Alliance to non-denominational)

For some it was the death of young people or peers:

I really struggled for a while with the death of a friend in high school. We prayed so hard, and it seemed God didn't hear us. (Loyal Believer 22, Pentecostal)

A camper I knew passed away in his sleep for no reason that I am aware of. (Loyal Believer 25, Baptist to Anglican)

In two cases, the death was that of child. The comments are short and moving:

Our son . . . died on Jan 6, 1997. (Loyal Believer 35, none to Free Evangelical)

The questions surrounding the death of a baby. (Loyal Believer 27, Presbyterian)

Some have struggled with chronic illness, physical or psychological, either in their own lives or in that of someone they love:

My wife's depression struggles; healing issues and struggling with God's care. (Loyal Believer 38, Baptist to Mennonite)

Going through a depression and feeling that God had abandoned me, thus not trusting him and giving up on him. (Loyal Believer 35, Anglican to Vineyard)

Recurring illness of a family member. (Loyal Believer 27, Baptist to non-denominational)

Personal psychological issues. (Loyal Believer 25, Christian and Missionary Alliance)

Other people have known abuse in their own lives and the lives of those near to them:

I struggled with how much physical abuse my sister's boyfriend (years ago) went through as a child. I could not reconcile a God of love with this. (Loyal Believer 30, Baptist to Christian and Missionary Alliance)

I was bullied and sexually assaulted in a Christian environment. (Loyal Believer 26, Anglican)

A non Christian friend was raped (by a stranger), then later beaten up by her boyfriend, then her sister was also raped and ended up having an abortion, then my same friend developed pre-cancerous cells in her cervix. (Loyal Believer 23, Anglican)

One thing that strikes me about these comments is that there is nothing Pollyannaish about them. Sometimes religious people will say things like, Oh, God knows what he's doing; it was a happy release; God's ways are mysterious, and so on. No, the responses to God given here are raw and honest. They say bluntly: We struggled with the idea of God's care, I gave up on God, it was difficult to endure, I could not reconcile this with a God of love, God didn't hear our prayer.

Most writers who dare to tackle "the problem of suffering" these days say that part of a healthy spiritual response to evil and suffering is to complain to God. They point to people in the Bible who did just that—Moses, Job, Jeremiah, the Psalmist, and others. Charles Ohlrich's book *The Suffering God* was the first to alert me to this:

In the prologue [to the Book of Job], God describes Job as a man of integrity. The violent expression of anger and doubt which follows . . . is not a denial of this integrity but an expression of it. Integrity and honesty go hand in hand . . . God respects this honesty above mindless submission.[2]

Many respondents have discovered the same thing—that the God they follow is not offended by their honesty, and that in the end their faith is strengthened, not destroyed, by being angry with God. One Returned Believer illustrates this paradox beautifully:

> I never considered walking away from God but I sure have been very angry at Him. There were times I remember screaming out at Him and making it clear we weren't on speaking terms. However, giving up on God . . . wasn't an option. The bad times in my life would have been so much worse without God to get me through, whether I was speaking to Him or not! (Returned Believer XX, Christian Missionary Alliance)

Another says: "In times of trouble I'm more likely to become angry with God and challenge him on my situation." (Loyal Believer 25, United)

For this and other reasons, several of them write about how their faith has been reinforced through these experiences:

> [Suffering] acted to increase my faith as I turned to God to help me through the death of my 1-year-old nephew who was seriously ill from birth. (Loyal Believer 28, Presbyterian to Anglican)

> Actually, I found that catastrophe brought me on my knees in front of Jesus. (Loyal Believer 26, Lutheran to Christian and Missionary Alliance)

> God has never let me down and actually it has been when struggling with bereavements and difficult issues that I have felt his presence most! (Loyal Believer 25, Congregational to Anglican)

---

2. Charles Ohlrich, *The Suffering God: Hope and Comfort for Those Who Hurt* (Downers Grove: InterVarsity Press, 1982), 22.

This [unspecified catastrophe] only managed to bring me closer to God as I was unwilling to talk to others so I went to God because I knew that He would never leave no matter what was happening. (Loyal Believer 23, none to Baptist)

I've never considered throwing in the Christian towel. In times of trouble I'm more likely to become angry with God, and challenge him on my situation—but I think this is a good thing because in these times my faith is in the forefront of my mind and for a time more tangible and real. (Loyal Believer 25, United)

These people's relationship with God is somewhat like a good marriage, where a couple has learned to weather the storms by expressing anger appropriately and working through the difficulties, rather than giving up on the relationship. I cannot help wonder how many who gave up on faith during times of suffering had not learned to face God with their anger and frustration, but gave up on faith instead. Did their churches and youth groups help them deal with the emotional component of suffering—or only with the intellectual question of why God allows suffering?

To change the analogy, these are people with a strong faith. But it is not the rigid strength of concrete, which can snap under the stress of an earthquake. No, this kind of faith is more like a mature oak tree, which has grown strong over time and has deep roots and thus can withstand the wind.

So how exactly has the faith of Loyal Believers changed over time?

HOW FAITH CHANGES

Those who write about this topic speak in terms of

- growing up
- thinking things out for themselves
- coming to appreciate complexity, and
- rejecting simplistic answers.

66

One says: "If we're not thinking, then we're not growing" (Loyal Believer 24, Baptist to Methodist). Another says she will continue to "morph [her] understanding of what Christianity means" (Loyal Believer 24, Anglican). In general, they speak of coming to appreciate more openness, more ambiguity, and more space for diversity.[3] Here is the kind of thing they say:

> My view of Christianity has changed over time, that is, my idea of what it means to be a Christian has changed. (Loyal Believer 31, Presbyterian)

> I guess I don't really see everything in black and white any more. (Loyal Believer 29, Baptist to Anglican)

As life changes, so the demands made on faith are different, and faith itself changes in response:

> I realize that I am making serious transitions in my life space. I can't rely on what 'worked' before because life is so different . . . I am in the process of finding new ways of connecting with God. This is hard . . . My faith looks very different now than it did when I was at camp. (Loyal Believer 26, Baptist to non-denominational)

THINKING FOR MYSELF

For some, going to camp as a teenager was the beginning of learning to think more broadly about Christianity, not least since there they mixed with Christians from many different denominations, sometimes for the first time:

> Pioneer was really a turning point for me in being able to go away from home and friends and think through issues for myself. (Loyal Believer 25, Congregational to Anglican)

---

3. James Fowler would describe this as the transition from Stage Four to Stage Five.

Camp was the first time I remember wrestling with issues for myself. (Loyal Believer 24, United)

At one point in processing the data from this survey, I invited respondents living in the Toronto area to attend a focus group. Eight responded, representing a range of years in the leadership program from 1986 and 1997. I asked them to comment on their experience of the development of their faith. One woman described the process of taking her "received faith" and making it her own in these terms:

When I was younger, I took a lot of what other people told me I was supposed to believe as a Christian, and so I accepted that. As I get older, I take the stuff I've been told, and I sift it all and apply it to my everyday world, and say, "Does that make sense?" I now have a belief system.

Others in the group agreed:

People need to look at God in a new way from the way they had growing up.

A Loyal Believer puts it this way:

If the unexamined life is not worth living,[4] then surely the same could be said for the unexamined faith? Surely it is the unexamined and blind faith . . . that is the first to throw in the towel when confronted with doubts and difficulties? (Loyal Believer 38, Anglican)

For some, this simply means acknowledging that God, faith and reality are more complicated than they ever dreamed. This group are the ones who say "my relationship with God" is the most important element in their ongoing faith, so it is worth noticing that even though God is a constant, the way they relate to God changes. It is like any other long-term relationship (between spouses, or

---

4. Socrates, *Apology,* 38a.

parents and children), where the basic commitment may remain the same, but the dynamics of the relationship need renegotiation from time to time in order for it to stay healthy.

Another respondent puts it this way:

> I feel more open to consider and accept different ways of
> believing in God. Lately I have felt that the church and many
> Christians try to put Christianity and God in a box to make it
> easier and more comfortable, when in fact it and he are difficult
> to understand. (Loyal Believer 38, Anglican)

The phrase "God in a box" suggests a kind of faith where all answers can be known and everything can be understood—within fixed limits. It also suggests a relationship that does not change. When we are young, it is important to see things that way: it gives us a sense of stability and security. Whether or not anyone actually tells us that is the way faith is, this is often the way it is heard and received. It requires a degree of maturity to admit, "Ultimately, I cannot understand everything, God is bigger than my mind can handle, and Christianity is more complex than I will ever grasp." Some say this kind of thing:

> One of the most significant things for me was understanding
> that I wouldn't understand it all (not in a passive, giving up
> kind of way, just in a realization of where faith begins). (Loyal
> Believer 23, Anglican)

For some at least, this is an exciting thing. There is a sense of discovering new dimensions to Christian faith which actually energizes the spiritual journey:

> [What has helped you stay in the Christian faith?] Belief that
> there is more to Christianity that I have not yet experienced.
> (Loyal Believer 26, nondenominational to Presbyterian)

VIOLENT OR GENTLE CHANGE?

Although there can be a sense of a joyous adventure about this, one focus group participant spoke about how having less certainty can be devastating:

> I was challenged in university in religious studies courses. The challenge caused me to re-evaluate, sift, broaden my belief system. My "God box" had been shattered.

Once again, here is the picture of a box—safe, rigid, and practical—but now it is being broken apart. Another person talks about "deconstruction" to make the same point:

> I have spent time deconstructing my beliefs to the point of having very little or no Christian beliefs, but that was in the spiritually safe environs of L'Abri[5] fellowship. The process . . . will always be ongoing. (Loyal Believer 32, Anglican to United)

To go through a phase of having no beliefs is very frightening. One writer suggests it is as traumatic as a shipwreck: the believer has to swim to shore and start life over.[6]

C.S. Lewis experienced a similar kind of breaking of the box after the death of his wife, and had to rethink how he could live with his new understanding of God. His conclusion was that God is behind this process of breakdown and re-formation, because our old ways of thinking about God are actually not good for us:

---

5. The L'Abri communities were begun by Francis and Edith Schaeffer in 1955. Their website describes them as "study centers . . . where individuals have the opportunity to seek answers to honest questions about God and the significance of human life. L'Abri believes that Christianity speaks to all aspects of life." (www.labri.org.)

6. Sharon Daloz Parks, *The Critical Years* (HarperCollins, 1986), 24–25.

My idea of God is not a divine idea. It has to be shattered time after time . . . Could we even say that this shattering is one of the marks of His presence?[7]

Not everybody experiences this kind of growth as violent or distressing, however. Some use the less dramatic imagery of building on foundations when they think about changes in their faith. They talk about how early influences such as family and camp helped them lay good foundations for their growth in faith. What they have chosen to build on that foundation, however, has been their choice, and may well be different:

Camp, IVCF etc. were very important in the past, but seem to have less of a role today. However, they provided me with a foundation upon which I practice my faith. (Loyal Believer 32, Anglican to Mennonite)

I think in my life overall, my parents were the biggest influence and contributors to my faith—helping me to get a good foundation on which to build—although my personal expression of faith and beliefs have deviated somewhat from theirs over the years. (Loyal Believer 34, Baptist to Anglican)

One person, who is in the process of becoming a Roman Catholic, uses different language again—that of a leisurely journey—to describe how the process is unfolding for her:

In the past few years I have felt that I am on a journey, learning as I go along, trying to live in the present moment. Sometimes the moment escapes me and then I get anxious about the past or the future. I have learned from reading and visiting [a retreat centre] that the heart is the place out of which I desire to live. Slowly and gently but surely I, with grace, follow Christ. (Loyal Believer 30, Methodist to Catholic)

---

7. C. S. Lewis, *A Grief Observed* (London: Faber and Faber 1961), 52. God, says Lewis, is "the great iconoclast."

People who speak about building on foundations and continuing on a journey see greater continuity between their original faith and their current faith than those who talk about "shattering." It would be interesting to know what makes the difference: whether it is something to do with the nature of the original faith, or the nature of the forces for change, or whether it is simply a difference of personality. In any case, both are authentic and important developments in faith. However growth takes place, many would agree with the Loyal Believer who wrote, "I continue to reconsider the way I believe."

CONSERVATIVE OR LIBERAL?

Some describe their spiritual growth as moving to a more "liberal" theology. Not many talk this way, however, in spite of the fact that most were originally from conservative churches. Probably the fact that more have moved from mainline churches to conservative ones than the reverse is also a factor here.

For those who do say they have moved towards the theological "left", sometimes this is through critical study of the Bible at university:

> I took a course in first year at university that took a look at the Old Testament from a historical perspective . . . It really challenged the way I had been taught . . . to look at things in black and white. After a month of so, I realized that I could not simply walk away from my faith, and I have landed with a somewhat more liberal view of things. (Loyal Believer 24, Anglican)

Others find that a traditional view of salvation (redemption only through Christ) pushes them to find an alternative:

> Universalist or inclusivist theologies make me feel like it wouldn't be a horrible thing to let go of "evangelical" conservatism, and embrace a less rigid interpretation of redemption. (Loyal Believer 30, Baptist to Mennonite)

Both of these make a distinction between rejecting faith and reinterpreting it. The first writer wants to keep her faith but with a "more liberal view"; the second still holds a belief in "redemption", but a "less rigid" one.

On other questions too, respondents do not want to reject their faith, but they do want to find a different way to understand and express it. I noticed this particularly on questions of sexuality. One writer is explicit about moving away from traditional Christian views on this subject—though again he makes clear that he is not leaving Christian faith itself:

> I also am kind of on the fence about some of those tenets that the Christian church professes ([about] homosexuality, premarital sex) and yet I still consider myself a Christian. (Loyal Believer 29, Baptist to Anglican)[8]

Another person is trying not to move away from Christian ethics but to bring her ethical views into line with the ultimate Christian standard—Jesus himself:

> These [conservative] stances have caused many of my gay friends to leave the church and their Christian faith. I feel hypocritical going to a church that would make them feel that they are sinners rather than take Jesus' approach and just love them. If what they are doing is sinful, I think God will help them through that. I don't think that it is my job, nor the church's job. (Loyal Believer 30, Baptist to Anglican)

One lesbian couple have moved out of the mainstream of Christian faith in order to be in a community that was accepting of their partnership. (They attend a Quaker meeting house.) They too

---

8. The fact that the writer equates conservative churches with "the Christian church" presumably means that, while growing up, he believed that his conservative church was the only truly "Christian" church.

continue to "respect the Christian story" but to interpret it in a more liberal way. One writes:

> Despite how easy and certain that [background] was, I would not want to go back to the controlled, tight person I was who was completely out of touch with her true emotions and identity. I am a much happier, healthier person today, and feel much more whole. I have a deeply meaningful spirituality that still respects the Christian story but does not depend on it. (Loyal Believer 29, Anglican to Quaker)

CORE AND CULTURE

Not every issue can be reduced to liberal-conservative or left-right shifts, however. Another way people speak of their development is in terms of learning to distinguish between "core Christianity," which they want to hold onto, and various cultural ways of expressing faith, which they sit light to:

> I have come to see myself as a "recovering evangelical." Organized Christianity, in particular the conservative church and its emphasis on "right thinking", have tempted me to throw out the baby with the bath water . . . I have come to think that much of what we label "Christian faith" is merely modernity / modern philosophy with an organized religion twist. I am sad when I see friends who have walked away from the b.s. of fundamental evangelical Christianity and in the process have walked away from Jesus. (Loyal Believer 36, Baptist to Presbyterian)

> I think that I have stayed within the Christian faith in spite of the evangelical Christian community. There is so much of a disconnect between the culture of the [evangelical] church and how I see God wanting us to interact with the world that in fact I no longer hold to much of what I once believed. Having said that, my core beliefs (limited though they may be) are still fundamentally biblical and "Christian"—and that is due to remarkable individuals and communities who were able to help me

find congruity between a biblical God, social responsibility and intellectual questions. (Loyal Believer 32, Anglican to United)

The question of distinguishing what is essential to Christian faith and what is just a temporary cultural expression of it, or a warped expression of it, is an ongoing struggle. One place where it comes to the fore is when people are confronted by another culture:

[I was challenged by] living on a First Nations reserve and being ASHAMED to be a Christian. Having to work through the process of what is truth and what is culture in both my world and theirs. As a result, I was really angry with "Christians" and wanted to dissociate myself from "them." I still struggle with this, often. Who am I? Who is the church? When it comes to judgment and truth, we are all fallen and desperately need to seek out truth and learn from one another. (Loyal Believer 27, Christian and Missionary Alliance to nondenominational)

GROWTH IN FAITH: AN ONGOING JOURNEY

Challenges to faith among this group have obviously been numerous and severe. They have experienced the limitations and brokenness of the Christian community. They have had horrible experiences of suffering. They have faced new intellectual and ethical dilemmas. Sharon Daloz Parks says about such developments in faith:

One becomes a young adult in faith when one begins to take self-conscious responsibility for one's own knowing, becoming and moral action—even at the level of ultimate meaning-making. This moment in the journey of faith does not typically occur until at least the age of seventeen, though for many people it emerges much later—or never.[9]

---

9. Parks, 77–78.

Some who responded to the survey have passed this point in their journey. I cannot help wondering whether there are some who have never made this transition of making their faith their own. It is difficult to tell. The answer is probably no, but certainly people will have changed in different ways, some more dramatic than others.

What does this mean for the church's ministry to young people? One thing youth workers and churches can do is to prepare them for this long journey, for the new vistas and the new difficulties ahead. This is not the same as forcing them to grow up prematurely. Nor is it a matter of being patronising about the fact that their present faith is immature. But leaders can sow seeds which will bear fruit later: by warning that the Christian life will not always be easy, by honouring older believers who have faced suffering and doubt, and by trying to draw distinctions between core faith and cultural expressions of it.

One of the younger respondents speaks warmly of her church for just this reason:

> I think my church does an excellent job of responding to young people. The leadership does not put on a pretense of having it all together or having it all figured out, but they share the truth of Christianity just as it is with the young people. I think it gives the young people a realistic picture of what it means to be a Christian and of how God works in one's life. (Loyal Believer 23, Pentecostal)

4

UNDER THE HOOD

How Loyal Believers Give Out, How They Take In

Loyal Believers are people who continue to follow Christ and to develop in their understanding and expression of faith. They do so in spite of frustrations with the church. In fact, they continue to be active—very active—in the churches of their choice. One thing is plain from their responses: they are not passengers in the life of these churches—they are the crew.[1] This adds a fresh edge to the question: What keeps you in Christian faith? Now I find I want to ask also: What sustains you and your faith when you are so active in church? Let us look first at what they actually do.

A RANGE OF MINISTRIES

Loyal Believers are involved in an amazing range of ministries in their churches. They were invited to check off their commitments from a short list, but then seventy-five wrote in further comments,

---

1. There were a few exceptions. One, who checked no boxes, commented: "Now I feel guilty. Oh well, at least you pointed out why I don't feel involved at my church." (Loyal Believer 26, Anglican to Baptist)

greatly expanding my list, not only in terms of what ministries they are involved in, but adding texture and context. The following is a taste of the diversity of the roles these respondents play in their churches:

- "I work in the church library"
- "[I am involved in] Stephen Ministries, which is basically lay counseling to hurting people"
- "We ran an outreach play group for children of single parents"
- "My primary calling in life is as a one-on-one evangelist in the business community."
- "Heavily involved with International Student Ministry"
- "Out of the Cold" (overnight hospitality for homeless people)
- "[I am] the Scripture Reader coordinator"
- "I am a leader in a Bible study group for those interested in learning more about the Christian faith but who are not necessarily Christians"
- "Collecting aid for an orphanage in Mexico"
- " Part of set-up service team (we meet in a school hall)"
- "I'm on the premises committee helping to maintain the building"
- "Helped out with retreat planning"
- "Oversee Food Bank"
- "Cleaning and maintenance"
- "Church's fundraising program for the Jubilee Initiative" (for the cancellation of international debt)
- "I am stage manager for the church Easter production"
- "I greet and count collection on a fairly regular basis, and run the PowerPoint projector when the other guy is away"
- "I am a mentor to a recent teenage believer in my church"
- "Working with charities providing a Christian response to children at risk internationally."
- "I designed and maintain the [church] website"
- "I sing in the bass section of the choir"
- "Halloween food drive"

- "I write dramas relevant to today's situations, direct, act, set up, etc."
- "I co-lead a snowboard ministry."

And last but not least:

- "I bring Tim Hortons coffee for the back row group."

Roughly 50% of these are what we might call "in-house" ministries for the maintenance of the church (librarian, finances, building maintenance), while the other 50% are oriented to the outside world (international students, Mexico, the food bank).

The biggest single group of write-in comments (11) was from those involved in professional ministry (in the sense that they are employed by a Christian organization such as a church)—pastor, youth pastor, Christian education director, student intern, church planter, and so on—so I have added them to the Figure 8 below.[2]

What this graph does not make clear, however, is how many Loyal Believers are involved in more than one ministry. These are people who give a great deal to the life of their churches. The following are typical:

> My wife and I are founders of a small house church, meeting on
> Saturday nights, as well as active in a more traditional church
> on Sundays. In the house church setting, I sometimes preach,

---

2. Some strange distinctions emerge when we compare denominational backgrounds. For example, those who identify with mainline churches, either now or in their growing up, were far more likely to be involved in preaching (17.5% of those who are now mainline and 22% of those used to be mainline and who are now conservative) than those who identify with conservative churches, now or in their growing up (8% for those who are still conservative and 4% for those who have switched to mainline). Those who grew up in conservative churches, however, are more likely to be involved in music ministry (just over 30%) than those who grew up mainline (just over 20%). Those who have switched from mainline churches to conservative churches are far less likely to be involved in a leadership role than others (2.4% compared with around 10%).

Figure 8: Ministries of Loyal Believers

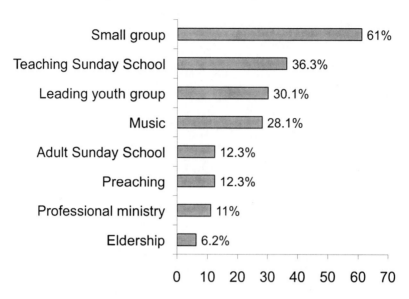

am involved in music and am considered an elder. (Loyal Believer 38, Baptist to non-denominational)

We have regular outreaches to those in the community; random acts of kindness, soccer camp, Vacation Bible School, Fall Carnival. We are planting a church—year 2.5. I have served on the leadership team and on the pastoral search team. (Loyal Believer 36, Anglican to Mennonite)

Elder: deacons' board and deacons' executive. Outreach programs: I have taught sessions on ecology and theology at my church and for church leaders in downtown Toronto. As well, I was on the Board representing [my denomination] on the taskforce on the churches and corporate responsibility. (Loyal Believer 36, Baptist)

I used to do Sunday School, and did a few sermons for the evening service. In the past, we ran an outreach play group for children of single parents. (Loyal Believer 30, Methodist to Catholic)

While such activism is gratifying for church leaders, it is possible for people to be too active in church, and to burn out. There is a warning note in an enthusiastic comment like this one: "There are times I feel I am over involved in the church. But there is nothing I would rather be doing" (Loyal Believer 36, Baptist). It is all too easy for an overworked pastor to hear the second sentence with a sense of relief, and not to hear the note of danger in the first.

One researcher found that among those who drop out of church life: "[t]he fact that some respondents were expected to make too many commitments influenced 47% to leave the church."[3] With that warning in mind, some respondents sound as though they are being over-stretched:

> We are asked to do more, but feel we can't. I feel there is a constant pressure to do and give more, and that we have to protect ourselves from cracking under the pressure. I often wish we could rest a little. I feel guilty wanting to rest because I know our church is small and needy. (Loyal Believer 37, Mennonite to Baptist)

> It is insane how many things you get involved with when you are truly comfortable at a church. I feel like a member of the family and so am willing to donate much of my time to the church. They are such a vital part of my life. I feel better just being around these people. God blesses us all so richly in allowing us to do His work. (Loyal Believer 26, Methodist to Baptist)

> Being in ministry and the expectations people put on you can be really hard. (Loyal Believer 25, Pentecostal to non-denominational)

Others have decided there are other priorities in their lives at this point:

---

3. Peter Brierley, quoted in Eddie Gibbs, *In Name Only: Tackling the Problem of Nominal Christianity* (Wheaton: Victor Books 1994), 291.

The truth is that we go to a church over 40 minutes away. I teach school and work for hours at night marking, and I have two little kids at home. There's just no time for me to do stuff like that. Now is not the time. (Loyal Believer 36, United to Anglican)

In chapter 9, I will return to this theme of busy-ness and potential burnout, as one of the things churches have to be on guard for.

HOW DO LOYAL BELIEVERS NURTURE THEIR SPIRITUAL LIFE? [4]

Something encourages Loyal Believers to continue on with their walk of faith, even though they are upfront about the fact that it is not always easy, and even though it is always developing and changing. They say that their relationship with God is the thing that keeps them faithful, but how is that relationship nurtured?

In order to probe this area, I asked: "Which, if any, of the following activities are you involved in which help you nurture your relationship with God?" The possibilities I offered were:

- Prayer
- Sunday worship
- Personal Bible study
- Small group
- Meditation
- Seeing a spiritual director

The results are to be seen in Figure 9. In wording the question, I was thinking mainly in terms of some of the traditional "spiritual

---

4. The figures for how Returned Believers nurture their spiritual life are almost identical. The one exception is in personal Bible study, which 73% of Loyal Believers rate as important or very important, compared with 63.4% of Returned Believers.

Figure 9: How do Loyal Believers
nurture their faith?

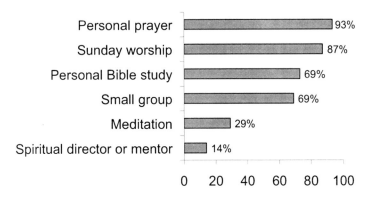

disciplines."[5] However, the additional comments people wrote in opened up a wide range of other options.

FRIENDS

I should not have been surprised to find that friends continue to be very important. No fewer than twenty-one write about the influence of friends—though, as before, these are not just casual acquaintances, but people who will hold one another spiritually accountable. This spiritual aspect of the relationships is made quite explicit time after time:

> Keep contact with friends who love God and have hearts that seek after him. (Loyal Believer 38, Christian Reformed)

> Two close friendships of fellowship, sharing, and accountability, related to our Christian faith specifically. (Loyal Believer 37, Associated Gospel Church to Pentecostal)

---

5. Anglicans rate personal prayer somewhat more highly than do Baptists (95.7% compared with 87.1%), while Baptists rate personal Bible study 11% more highly than do Anglicans (67.7% compared with 56.5%).

Sharing with family and friends what God is doing in my life, and hearing what He is doing in theirs. (Loyal Believer 30, Baptist to Vineyard)

Conversations with friends about their understanding and experience of God and how Christianity affects their life. I find friends—peers and adult mentor types—to be the most helpful in encouraging me to pursue my relationship with God. (Loyal Believer 26, non-denominational to Presbyterian)

My friends and I act as accountability partners for each other, kinda calling each other on behaviours, and praising the good stuff we do. (Loyal Believer XX, Christian and Missionary Alliance)

SMALL GROUPS[6]

In many cases, these friendships are somewhat formalized into small groups that meet regularly. Some are for specific constituencies, such as mothers, or to focus on specific ministries, such as healing or prophecy, or to talk about specific issues, such as finances and family. All go beyond a purely formal time of Bible study, and involve sharing of personal issues and (in some cases) spending time together outside the regular gathering.

I am a part of a community moms prayer group and that nurtures my relationship [with God]. (Loyal Believer 38, Presbyterian to Baptist)

I have a very good group of friends who I see outside of church and would do anything for. (Loyal Believer 37, Baptist to Anglican)

---

6. Baptists are much more likely to be involved in a small group than Anglicans (64.5% compared with 43.5%). I suspect this is due to the Christendom syndrome I mentioned earlier which afflicts many mainline Christians.

I'm involved in two different small groups—one for ladies and one on prophecy. (Loyal Believer 35, Baptist to Associated Gospel Church)

Personal growth is an area I feel has suffered in my life for lack of time (young family) and now want to focus more time and commitment to this area so have joined a small group Bible study. (Loyal Believer 33, Baptist)

Have started a small men's group of five men, to hold each other accountable and discuss matters of faith, family and finances. Additional activities include regular readings by Christian authors. (Loyal Believer 33, Christian Reformed to Associated Gospel Church)

I have been in a woman's accountability/prayer group for the past 3 years and it has been amazing. We really grow together, support each other, and pray for each other through all phases of life. I believe accountability is absolutely essential for Christians. My husband is in a men's accountability group. (Loyal Believer 25, Christian and Missionary Alliance)

I love my small group and will likely remain in one for my entire life. (Loyal Believer 24, United)

Two go so far as to say that their small group experience is more important than Sunday morning worship in the wider community:

For me the most meaningful worship experiences are in a house church setting on Saturday nights, not in the larger group on Sunday mornings. (Loyal Believer 38, Baptist to non-denominational)

Small groups have been paramount to keeping me strong in faith as opposed to attending church weekly. (Loyal Believer 37, Anglican to Christian and Missionary Alliance)

Small groups of Christians have always been a part of the Christian church at its most vital, from the days of the New Testament through the birth of the monastic movement to the Methodist movement in the eighteenth century and the charismatic movement of the 1960s and 1970s. Indeed, some would argue that much of the ethical instruction in the New Testament assumes the kind of close relationships which are only possible in a small group. As a result, it is not surprising that Loyal Believers rate small groups as such an important part of their continuing faith.

MENTORS AND/OR SPIRITUAL DIRECTORS

I added the question about a spiritual director partly out of curiosity to discover how far people from evangelical backgrounds had begun to explore the spiritual resources of other traditions. Partly as a result, there was some confusion about the question. One person asked bluntly, "What is a spiritual director?" Others asked, "Is this the same as a mentor?"

It is true that there is often overlap between what is meant by spiritual direction (in the Catholic tradition) and what is meant by mentoring or discipling (which is by and large more Protestant). One broad distinction, however, can be that a mentor often has a more intentional agenda or curriculum in mind for what the "disciple" needs to learn, whereas a spiritual director is more inclined to attend to whatever is going on within the directee's relationship with God. (Ironically enough, this means that the "director" is less likely to be directive.[7]) One person actually says:

> My spiritual director is very kind, but doesn't ever give me a
> kick in the butt when I get slack in my spiritual life, and I need
> that from time to time. (Loyal Believer 25, Anglican)

Having said that, the distinction seems to be blurred in several of the responses that follow.

---

7. The common misunderstanding of spiritual direction is illustrated by the response of the person who thinks a spiritual director would give "prescriptions about what I should be doing in my spiritual life."

Some respondents identified with the term "spiritual director" and were clearly familiar and comfortable with the term. I was not surprised to find that 17.4% of Anglicans say they are seeing a spiritual director, compared with 6.5% of Baptists. Anglicans are in this respect closer to the Catholic tradition. However, some of the most enthusiastic comments came from people in churches which have not traditionally been interested in spiritual direction:

> I have seen a spiritual director—it was wonderful! (Loyal Believer 36, Baptist)

> I would love to be seeing a spiritual director right now but haven't connected with one in this new community. I have found spiritual direction helpful in the past. (Loyal Believer 30, Presbyterian to Baptist)

Others equate spiritual director with mentor, and at least four describe a yearning for this kind of relationship, whatever its name:

> I currently do not have a mentor. I would love to have one as I have had at other points in my life and I continue to pray that God would provide another for me when the time is right. (Loyal Believer 38, Baptist)

> I am interested in knowing more about the idea of spiritual directors. I had a few men in my life whom I considered to be mentors when I was 16-21. I have longed for that since but have not found it. (Loyal Believer 36, Baptist to Presbyterian)

> I really wish I had a spiritual director. I have older Christian friends I hang out with occasionally but there is no one in my life I can REALLY reflect with/talk to about my relationship with God. (Loyal Believer 32, Presbyterian)

> I wish I could check "Seeing a spiritual director" because I have been meaning to initiate this for some time. (Loyal Believer 28, Baptist to Anglican)[8]

---

8. In many areas, there exist directories of spiritual directors, listing their

One woman explains one of the keys to effective mentoring like this:

> I think one of the main things for me in nurturing my relationship with God was finding a woman who was older than me, a more experienced Christian, who had been through a lot of the same things I went through. And seeing how God helped her through them. (Loyal Believer 24, Baptist to non-denominational)

In such a relationship, there is a natural overlap, at least for some, between spiritual direction (or mentoring) and counseling:

> I have had a spiritual director for the past year. She has been instrumental in opening up of the Pandora's box of pain that was in me, allowing me to feel more freedom. (Loyal Believer 30, Methodist to Catholic)

And two Presbyterians and one Baptist who are on the staff of churches have a mentoring relationship with their senior pastor:

> Regular theological reflection with senior minister. (Loyal Believer 34, Presbyterian)

> It's not a "spiritual director" per se, but my meetings with my supervisor in my church certainly fall into this category. (Loyal Believer 32, Presbyterian)

> My mentor is the youth pastor that I work with at Church. He has had 20 years of experience in youth ministry. (Loyal Believer 24, Christian and Missionary Alliance to Baptist)

These comments talk about people's relationships with other believers—friends, small groups, mentors, spiritual directors. But

---

training, experience, and particular interests. For people in Ontario, such a directory may be obtained from www.spiritualdirectors.on.ca or Spiritual Directors of Ontario, 46 Flanders Road, Guelph ON, N1G 1V9.

particularly in Protestantism there has long been an emphasis on a "personal relationship" with God. How does that show up in these responses?

PERSONAL DEVOTIONS

In the evangelical stream of Protestantism, a traditional part of spiritual growth is the daily "quiet time"—a time alone, focusing on Bible reading and prayer. For many people who grew up in the evangelical tradition, this has remained a habit:

> The most important part of my relationship with God is my relationship with God, meaning that I feel that God's been teaching me the importance of spending time with Him daily, whether in reading the Bible, praying, journaling, listening (meditating), walking in nature, etc. (Loyal Believer 32, Baptist)

> I pray and read the Word daily. (Loyal Believer 30, Presbyterian to Anglican)

There are far more, however, who talk about a regular "quiet time" as a difficult thing. No spiritual discipline is easy, of course, particularly the solitary ones. Twelve respondents take the trouble to describe the difficulties they have in trying to be faithful in their practice of the "quiet time":

> I am still working on my own devotions. This is something I have always struggled with. When I do them I love it. But it gets skipped a lot when I am busy—which seems to be a lot. (Loyal Believer 32, Christian Reformed)

> I am currently struggling with prayer and reading the Bible on my own regularly (what we used to call "quiet time"). It is one of those things that (as St. Paul put it) I know I should do but I do not do. (Loyal Believer 31, Baptist to Congregational)

When I can get into a routine of daily devotion I recognize an immediate improvement in my personal relationship with God. (Loyal Believer 28, Presbyterian to Anglican)

Others simply complain that "My prayer life is weak" or that "Prayer is hard and usually feels fruitless" or that "None of this happens as often as I wish it would."

My hunch is that this personal discipline, while very valuable, needs to be supplemented, even replaced at times, with others. For example, some write about finding help in their relationship with God through such things as:

INVOLVEMENT IN MINISTRY

Ministry might seem like the antithesis of nurture. If nurture is like eating, isn't ministry like the exercise you can only do if you eat properly? Apparently it is not as simple as that. Several say that being involved in ministry is itself nurturing. When asked, "Which . . . activities are you involved in which help you nurture your relationship with God?" one replies simply: "Evangelism"! Another makes the connection like this:

I have had many opportunities to attempt to explain my faith, which has helped sharpen it. (Loyal Believer 25, United to Baptist)

Others write more broadly about growing through ministry:

Ministry forces me to depend totally on God and that deepens my relationship with Him. (Loyal Believer 30, Anglican to Christian and Missionary Alliance)

Involved in church activities that work towards social justice in our community (protests, collecting used clothing, strategizing around homelessness). (Loyal Believer 28, United to Quaker)

Being involved in ministry has been a major thing that I think has kept me in touch with God, relying on him. This led to growth and maturity in Christ. (Loyal Believer 26, Anglican to Associated Gospel Church)

Active involvement in faith-based social justice work. (Loyal Believer 26, Anglican)

The Letter of James says that "Faith without works is dead."[9] Sometimes when people feel that their faith has "gone dead," it is because they are not doing any faith-based "works."[10] These people have obviously discovered the corollary that doing Christian "works" actually helps to give life to one's faith.

PERSONAL AND CORPORATE

Others have discovered spiritual health in moving from personal nurture to corporate nurture and back again:

Improving my personal time with God is key, but for me my faith has been strengthened and reaffirmed when I spend time with other Christians. (Loyal Believer 31, Baptist)

I pray and read the Word daily. I am involved in a weekly, small group Bible study. (Loyal Believer 30, Presbyterian to Anglican)

Definitely my personal quiet time has been the most important part, but I would also have to say that discussion with my peers about what we're learning, the sermon, etc., has been very valuable. (Loyal Believer 25, Christian and Missionary Alliance)

I suspect that, for all believers, there are times when our personal awareness of God is weak and struggling, and then we need to turn to the community for strength. This is not a sign of weakness but simply an admission of reality. We are not created to be "lone

---

9. James 2:26.

10. I am indebted for this insight to the Rev. John Freeth of Cape Town, South Africa.

ranger" believers. Yet at other times, our own sense of God is strong, and that enriches what we are able to bring to the community. In this way the community and the personal have a symbiotic relationship, each giving to the other, each feeding off the other. Dietrich Bonhoeffer expressed the balance this way: "Only in the fellowship do we learn to be rightly alone and only in aloneness do we learn to live rightly in the fellowship." [11]

OTHER SOURCES OF NURTURE

In spite of the traditional evangelical emphasis on the personal "quiet time," most people I heard from do not rely on this alone for spiritual nurture. Indeed, the list of resources they draw on is quite remarkable. They include receiving Holy Communion, listening to sermons, journaling, fasting, personal retreats, Alpha, and formal theological studies.

Others say they receive significant spiritual help from the arts (painting and photography), music, parenting and (perhaps surprisingly) yoga.

Eleven speak of the importance of spiritual reading, apart from the Bible. (This is a group of university graduates, so this fact is hardly surprising.)

Under this same heading of nurture, others comment:

> I find that I love to sing Christian music so I joined the choir.
> (Loyal Believer 38, Baptist)

> My own academic work deals with Christianity and Literature, and I find that my studies and writings have continually fed my spiritual development. (Loyal Believer 38, Anglican)

> Reading the Bible stories, praying with and explaining Jesus to my own children. (Loyal Believer 33, Anglican)

---

11. Dietrich Bonhoeffer, *Life Together* (New York: Harper and Brothers, 1954), 77-78.

Books, workbooks and counseling for specific issues have
made an enormous difference in my ability to accept God's love
for me and build a relationship with him. (Loyal Believer 31,
Anglican to Free Methodist)

Everyday life!! (Loyal Believer 27, Anglican)

Devotions with my husband. (Loyal Believer 25, Baptist to
Anglican)

Talking with my dad. (Loyal Believer 23, Pentecostal)

It appears that nobody relies on just one source of spiritual
nurture, any more than a healthy diet consists of one kind of food.
Many people list four or five of the influences listed above. Nor, presumably, are these forms of nurture always equally valuable. Many
are helped from one source for a time, then move on to another, and
maybe return to the first at a later date. Variety in spiritual nurture
is as important as in physical nurture.

Youth groups which help their members develop a range of
spiritual disciplines will be equipping their members for the long
journey ahead.

WHERE ARE THEY HEADING?

I gave Loyal Believers an option which read, "I have never seriously
considered giving up being a Christian." I was interested to find that
two-thirds of this them (65.2%) checked this box. Although, as we
have seen, they write about major challenges to their faith, at the
same time, most of these reaffirm their convictions about the faith-
fulness of God, the reality of God, and so on. More than one refers
to the words of the Apostle Peter:

I have a verse on my fridge that reads: "You do not want
to leave too, do you?" Jesus asked the twelve. Simon Peter

answered him, "Lord, to whom shall we go? You have the words of eternal life."[12] (Loyal Believer 24, Christian Reformed)

As before, these are clearly not clichés but deeply held convictions, won over a period of testing. For these people at least, none of the challenges was strong enough to bring them to the point of thinking about giving up their faith.

The other one-third, presumably, did think about it, but decided there were strong enough reasons for staying within church and faith—some of which they wrote about in the previous chapter. For example:

> I've been through the tough questions. I think I will now hold onto my faith from here on, come what may. (Loyal Believer 32, Presbyterian)

> Sometimes I think it would be easier not to be a Christian, but then I realize how drastically my life would change . . . I realize that Christianity is the invisible glue that holds it all together. (Returned Believer 31, United to Baptist)

But what of future challenges? Some are not so sure what might happen. Thirty or so say that they expect their faith to be tested by the loss of loved ones. The following is typical:

> I suppose if anything happened to my husband or my new daughter . . . but I do not think I would ever give it up completely—just hibernate for a while and adjust my view somewhat. (Loyal Believer 34, Baptist to Anglican)

> I could see a personal tragedy being a difficult thing to work through with my Christian faith. As humans we look for answers when there may be none that we will understand, and that is a difficult position to accept. (Loyal Believer 27, Associated Gospel Church to Baptist)

---

12. John 6:68

However, as we have seen, the experience of those who have suffered is that it can actually strengthen faith. Some therefore feel that because they have coped with tragedy already they know their faith will see them through future difficulties:

> Maybe if I lost one of my children [I would lose my faith]. I DID lose my mom, and found God a huge strength in surviving that. I hate death and have some really big issues with it, but my issues are not with God. He didn't make death—he beat it. Thank heaven for that. (Loyal Believer 36, United to Anglican)

Other Loyal Believers think an experience of personal failure might cause them to give up:

> I feel like the guilt of my own sin, or the fear that I have strayed too far from God, would make me feel hesitant and shameful in coming back and seeking his forgiveness, if I felt I'd gone too far and couldn't go back. (Loyal Believer 23, Pentecostal)

Another group (about a dozen) recognizes that the hassles of church might eventually become too much for them and drive them away. For example, one writes:

> I think if I get to a point where I become sufficiently disillusioned with the Christian community—its conservatism, apathy or hypocrisy—it could push me into a place where I don't want to actively identify myself a Christian. (Loyal Believer 33, Baptist to Anglican)

Judging from the experience of those who have in fact dropped out (and in some cases returned), they are right: this is the factor that most often causes people to leave church—and sometimes faith itself. Even then, some make a distinction between personal faith and church involvement:

> There are things that could make me lose faith in Christians, but not in Christ. (Loyal Believer 27, Baptist)

This distinction will crop up again when we consider those who have dropped out of church life (either presently or in the past) but who continue to consider themselves Christians.

A further group (another dozen) say their faith would be shaken if what are for them the spiritual and theological foundations of faith were destroyed. These say, for instance, that they might lose their faith:

> If significant pillars of the faith were undermined such as the authenticity of scripture, the historicity of Christ's death and resurrection, etc. (Loyal Believer 33, non-denominational)

> There would have to be overwhelming intellectual and theological evidence against Christianity to make me consider leaving it: and that simply won't happen. (Loyal Believer 31, Associated Gospel Church)

More than one acknowledge that there will always be questions: "Various situations cause me to question why again and again"; "I feel like the older I get the more questions I have." For Loyal Believers as a whole, however, the majority view is expressed by the person who wrote, "I'm in it for the long haul!"

These then are the stories of those who have never departed from the fold. They have clearly explored the limits of that fold, and found them much broader and more flexible than they knew when they were teenagers. They have found ways of contributing to the ministry of the church with energy and imagination. Faith has not been an easy option for them, but they have persevered and found ways to grow and evolve in faith. And, in spite of not knowing what life may throw at them, they are modestly confident that they will continue in faith, and indeed, that their faith will enable them to cope with whatever comes.

What, however, of those who have moved away from church and given up their faith? Was their experience of faith different, and if so, how and why? The following chapter will look at these respondents and their stories.

5

U-TURNS

Why Do Former Believers Leave Faith?

Barb grew up in a conservative Free Methodist home, and always accepted the faith as her parents taught it to her. When she was a teenager, however, they were uncomfortable with the questions she asked about faith, and discouraged conversation about it. The youth group was fun, but when she asked questions, the youth leader just encouraged her to pray more. During the leadership training program at camp, she felt she had a breakthrough in terms of faith, but then, when she went on to university, she found the Christians she met legalistic and joyless, and found herself more in sympathy with non-Christians students who were thoughtful, compassionate, and more respectful of her as a woman. After graduation, she decided to work overseas for a relief agency, and while in Latin America, heard such awful stories about the history of missions there that she found herself more embarrassed than ever to have had involvement with the church. These days, she considers herself a spiritual person with a belief in an Ultimate Being, but is agnostic about what can be known about that being. She cannot imagine any circumstances in which she would want to return to Christian faith. Relations with her family are warm, but spiritual topics are simply avoided.

Fourteen of my respondents no longer consider themselves Christians, and are not involved in church or any other Christian activities. This is a small number so I do not want to draw sweeping conclusions from their comments. At the same time, their voices need to be heard, not least because what they say is both thought-provoking and chastening for the church.[1]

WHO ARE THE FORMER BELIEVERS?

The largest group of Former Believers are (or were) Baptists: five out of the fourteen. Presbyterians account for a further two, and the United Church for two. Twelve went to university, two to community or other colleges. Like most people who leave church and faith, the majority (13 out of 14) gave up their Christianity between the ages of 19 and 22, that is, during university and college years. (For the fourteenth person, leaving took place over five years, between the ages of 25 and 30.) The way one person describes the transition speaks for many:

> [I] stayed involved with my youth group and church until I was 18 (easy break when I moved away for university) [The process took] Maybe two years, the last year of high school and the first year of college. (Former Believer 23)

Many young Christians going to university are helped by campus ministries and chaplaincies. Of the Former Believers who went to university, however, only four were involved in a campus ministry (in each case it was IVCF), although there were large, lively groups on most campuses they went to. I suspect that those who did not join a group had already begun to move away from faith by that time (like the respondent just cited) and were not interested in campus fellowship.

---

1. Because the sample is so small, I will use simple numbers rather than percentages throughout this chapter.

WHY DID THEY LEAVE?

Those who identified themselves as Former Believers were offered these options as to why they stopped believing:

- The influence of peers who did not believe as you did
- Having too many difficult unanswered questions about the Christian faith
- Hypocrisy among Christians
- A catastrophe (e.g. incurable disease, accidental death) among those close to me
- Finding a partner who was not a Christian
- Feeling that I could no longer accept the exclusive claims of Christianity
- Lifestyle choices which differed from those expected in your Christian community, in areas such as alcohol use or sexual behaviour
- The need to be different from my parents
- Discovering that I was gay/lesbian
- Negative Christian role models (e.g. pastors, parents)
- Feeling that God had let me down (e.g. unanswered prayers)
- Moving away from significant Christian community
- Church seemed irrelevant to the questions of everyday life
- Disagreeing with various ethical beliefs in the church, e.g. abortion, euthanasia, homosexuality
- Feeling that my relationship with God was not real
- Dissatisfaction with Christianity's answers to the big questions of life
- Other (please specify)

Because so few filled out this particular survey, it should not surprise us that some of the options were not chosen by anybody. Out of the boxes that were checked, however, some were selected by 9 or 10 respondents, which is a large proportion of this group. (See Figure 10.)

The exclusiveness of Christian faith emerges as the strongest concern, followed closely by two kinds of problem with the church—hypocrisy among Christians, and ethical disagreements with positions commonly held among churches. The comments people wrote in explain more of what they mean.

Christian exclusiveness

Four Former Believers write about their problem with Christian claims to exclusiveness. They are likely to say things like "No one religion has a corner on the truth," so that for them other faiths are just as valid as Christianity:

> I don't think there's ONE way to heaven. For me, the lessons
> in the Bible are a good blue print for life—doing good, treating
> others well, generosity, self improvement, accountability, etc.
> But spirituality is individual and as long as the basics are there,
> I think we're all on the right track. (Former Believer 29)

> I feel that there is no difference between religions except a
> different human attempt to describe the unknown. I believe in
> a god but don't believe that any religion should distinguish one
> god from a god in every species. All differences are the creation
> of the human mind and are useless as they cause war and
> conflict. (Former Believer 23)

> I think Christianity is only one interpretation, and while it's
> totally beautiful and useful in its pure form, it's too often
> distorted and people forget that so many of the words and
> concepts we use are analogies. (e.g. God is LIKE a father, God
> isn't a HE or a Father per se). While I still totally believe in the
> Divine and the spiritual world, I couldn't reconcile myself to
> the Christian interpretation—it seemed too narrow and restric-

Figure 10: Factors causing Former Believers
to leave (numbers out of 14 indicating "Important" or
"Very important")

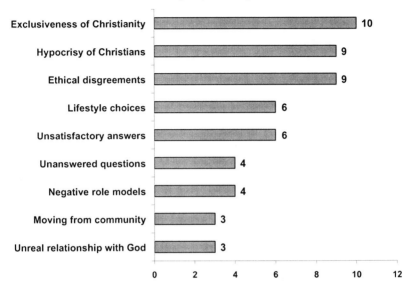

tive and too focused on a few things at the exclusion of others.
(Former Believer 23)

Why do I need such a narrow and patriarchal system to connect
with the divine? (Former Believer 23)

What saddens me is that these Former Believers have apparently
not come across Christians who take a different approach to this
difficult question. There are many Christians who would describe
themselves as traditional, orthodox, or evangelical, who would take
a more positive view of other religions than the one that has turned
these Former Believers off. C. S. Lewis is probably the most popular

writer about "traditional" Christianity who has affirmed the truth in other religions—even though he still sees Jesus as unique.[2]

Loyal Believers also rated this a significant challenge to their faith. It comes third, after hypocrisy in the church, and feeling that their relationship with God was unreal. Yet for them it was not enough to push them away from faith. My guess is that in many cases they discovered less exclusive ways of thinking about this issue, such as that of C. S. Lewis.

The challenge that comes first for Loyal Believers, however, is only third on the list for Former Believers:

Problems with church

Perhaps surprisingly, only five of the fourteen Former Believers talk about being disillusioned with church, naming such problems as closed-mindedness, judgementalism, hypocrisy, and racism. However, the language they use is stronger than those of Loyal Believers or Absent Believers on the same issues. It makes me wonder whether these five have been more badly hurt than people in the other groups, but I do not have enough information to draw such conclusions. In any case, some of the stories told by Loyal Believers or Absent Believers are fairly horrifying in any case, as we shall see.

It is easy for church folk to become defensive of the church and try to explain away stories like these as "just a misunderstanding" or "the impatience of youth." But Former Believers give such specific details of their experience that they cannot be explained away so easily. These stories carry the ring of truth.

---

2. Lewis talks about this issue particularly in *Mere Christianity* and *The Last Battle*. I discuss this issue in my book *Evangelism for 'Normal' People* (Augsburg Fortress, 2002). A fuller treatment is Clark Pinnock's *A Wideness in God's Mercy* (Zondervan, 1992), and a more academic treatment is Terrance Thiessen's *Who Can Be Saved? Reassessing Salvation in Christ and World Religions* (InterVarsity Press, 2004).

For example, some speak with legitimate anger of the unwillingness of family and church to discuss difficult issues:

> In my family [Christianity] had the effect of closing areas of inquiry, activity, even discussion, that would perhaps have been better left open and explorable . . . I am looking for answers elsewhere at the moment. (Former Believer 37)

> The church and my family treated me really poorly when I began to question blind faith. They tried to use control and scare tactics. They judged me, then they ostracized me. My non-Christian friends accepted me for who I was. (Former Believer 29)

It seems very sad to me that, in a religion which claims to worship the Creator of everything and the source of all truth, there are questions that cannot be asked. There was even a popular book called *All Truth is God's Truth.* [3] You might think that, where people believe that God is into truth, questions of truth could be pursued freely and openly—even when the answer might sometimes be, "I really don't know, but that's a great question."

Further, to use "control and scare tactics" would seem to be quite contrary to the spirit of Christianity and Jesus in particular. God clearly gives people the freedom to believe and choose paths that he does not approve of. Christian parents will try to imitate God's methods of parenting, even though it can be painful—for God as well as for us. What is more, Jesus who shows us God invites people to respond freely to his invitation to discipleship, so again trying to force people to believe undermines the nature of Christianity. Sub-Christian strategies are hardly going to make joyful, mature believers.

---

3. Arthur F. Holmes, *All Truth is God's Truth* (Grand Rapids: Eerdmans, 1977)

Lack of conviction about Christianity

I was interested to discover that four Former Believers say that perhaps their faith was shallow in the first place, although I would never want to suggest that this was the case for every Former Believer:

> My departure was more shallow, or my beliefs were more shallow to begin with. I describe the departure as simply 'walking away'. (Former Believer 37)

> The journey was not all that long as I don't think that I was ever overly convinced of my Christianity. (Former Believer 32)

> [I was] 18 years old, though my "faith" was not often something that I would consider to be a primary focus in my life. (Former Believer 29)

> I'd say that I was never really in it and I'm not all the way out the door now. If you want to be technical, I didn't have a lot of faith to lose. (Former Believer 24)

What is sad here is that many older Christians (and I realise I may have been one of them) who came into contact with these young people probably assumed that they were doing fine in their faith simply because they had Christian families, or were involved in their youth group, or went to a Christian camp. It may be wishful thinking to think that if someone had asked them, "So, how are you doing in your faith?" or "What are you finding tough in Christianity?" a conversation might have begun which would have led to a different outcome.

I couldn't help noticing too that ten Former Believers say nothing about Christian mentors, which we know to have been crucial for other groups. Of the other four, one does mention a mentor, but only in the context of being let down by that person, and three others speak of a failure among their Christian role models. Nor can we plead that they are from a tradition that did not encourage mentoring: the largest number of Former Believers were Baptist churches where other respondents did find mentors.

Some youth groups create intentional mentoring networks, linking up youth group members with mature believers in the congregation. Offering that service to young people can certainly help to plug the unintended gaps in their pastoral care.

The problem of suffering

Perhaps surprisingly, thirteen out of the fourteen Former Believers check the box which indicates this was "Not important" in their movement away from faith. Only one mentions the problem of suffering, and even then it is stated as a theoretical question rather than a personal story:

> Why is there suffering in the world when God is love? (Former Believer 23)

The majority of Loyal Believers and Absent Believers who mention the problem of suffering describe a specific instance of suffering in their lives or their families' lives. This is not to say that Former Believers have not suffered: it is clear that several have. Yet when it comes to describing why they gave up Christian faith, they do not mention this as a factor.

Many people assume that suffering is the main reason people give up believing in an all-powerful, all-loving God. Yet for these Former Believers, at least, it was not the issue that drove them away from belief. In fact, judging from the comments of Loyal Believers and Returned Believers, the paradox is that suffering seems to make them more likely to stay in the faith. I would argue that, while Christianity does not give a full "answer" to the problem, it does give clues, and, more importantly, it gives resources for responding to suffering.[4]

---

4. One of the best books I have found on this subject is Peter Kreeft's

THE PROCESS OF LEAVING

I was interested to know what the experience of leaving the church community was like. Was it fast or slow? Easy or painful? Did anybody realize what was happening? The majority (9) say that leaving was an easy thing to do, half (7) say it was a gradual process.[5]

Half of the respondents (7) say that their leaving faith was a concern for other people. Former Believers describe the tension and pain the process caused for them and their families very poignantly. It says a great deal for their courage that they were willing to keep going down this road:

> I tried to avoid addressing my change in a clear way with
> Christian parents, in order to minimize the motivation to change
> for rebellious reasons. I think I was able to achieve this, even
> though I do reject the way my parents practice their faith.
> (Former Believer 37)

> [It was] about a decade before I could be honest with people and
> family about my beliefs. For example, I STILL have difficulty
> causing the kind of distress to my grandparents which would
> result from a frank discussion in this area. (Former Believer 37)

> My parents were disapproving, but my LIT friends were not.
> (Former Believer 29)

Making Sense out of Suffering (Servant Books, 1986). Narratives such as John Terpstra's *The Boys* (Gaspereau Press, 2005) and Alan Paton's *Cry, the Beloved Country* (Penguin, 1958) give powerful accounts of Christians responding to suffering in everyday life.

5. Other research has found the same: "[Leavers] indicated a gradual process of reflection, questioning and withdrawal which lasted many months or years prior to their decision to leave" (Alan Jamieson, *A Churchless Faith: Faith Journeys Beyond the Churches* [London: SPCK, 2002], 32); see also Hoge: "Normally, there was a time of disenchantment or boredom that caused the person gradually to pull away." (Bromley, 92).

Sometimes my parents' friends make me feel so small and
inferior and tell me that I should have stayed with my abusive
husband [because] "marriage is a covenant between [the couple
and] God" . . . Sorry, but I think my daughter and I are much
better off now. I should be respected for the decision I made,
even if they don't agree, but I'm not. (Former Believer 26)

Jesus warned that faith in him might divide families,[6] so on one
level these comments are not surprising. Nevertheless, this does not
mean that all such splits are ones he would approve of, particularly
when there appears to be a lack of understanding and compassion
on the parental side. Whatever the case, one can feel the pain that
this parting of the ways has caused for everybody.

There is one respondent who manages to find positive aspects in
the disagreements with his family:

The change in the family dynamic is an ongoing source of
energy for exploring our varying views on the Christian faith.
Though there is rarely full agreement, I suspect there is hope for
change on both sides. (Former Believer 37)

I am reminded again that this survey is only a snapshot in time.
The last word has not been written and cannot be written. There is
almost always the possibility of progress, if not towards agreement,
at least towards reconciliation and new understanding. The positive
attitude in this last comment offers a glimpse of hope, in some cases
anyway.

The same is true of some of the comments Former Believers
make about friendships.

WHAT HAPPENS TO FRIENDSHIPS?

A small number of Former Believers keep up warm relationships
with Christian friends, or would like to do so:

---

6. E.g. Luke 12:51-53.

I do occasionally see several friends from camp and usually we enjoy each other's company, although I know several do not agree with my belief system, but usually we can discuss without hurting each other's feelings. (Former Believer XX)

I would be in contact with more camp friends if I lived closer to Ontario. (Former Believer 29)

I wish I could say that I actually saw more of them, but time and distance are hard to deal with. (Former Believer 24)

Others find friendships have cooled and become uncomfortable and formal:

I often feel awkward around Christians, because I know that they're concerned for my non-Christian-ness, and that they disagree with a lot of my attitudes and lifestyle choices. I feel judged—though I know Christians always say they don't judge, they still make opinions and form ideas about other people's choices and lifestyles. I don't want them to pray for me, it feels condescending, or like they're not really respecting my life choices and though I would like to be close with them and discuss personal things in the same way and even pray together, I don't want them to feel like they could convert me. (Former Believer 23)

There are few feelings, just a polite hello if we ever bump into one another. (Former Believer 38)

Once again, I think of C.S. Lewis' observation that friends are brought together by having things in common.[7] Once those commonalities have been eroded, the chances of the friendship surviving diminish, particularly if the friendship was forged in one's teens, when the majority of life changes are still ahead.

---

7. C.S. Lewis *The Four Loves*, 58–59

REFLECTIONS ON LEAVING

Former Believers were asked how they reflect on the time when they were Christians.[8] Nine choose the option, "It was a good experience at the time, but I was young." Only three believe that "I was simply going with the crowd and not thinking for myself." Nobody chose the option, "I'm not sure how it happened: I haven't given it much thought." In other words, it has been a subject for much reflection.

They were also asked about a range of emotions they might feel when they think back:

Anger

Three say they feel anger about their experience:

> I have not shaken off my enduring anger toward some fundamentalist church officials I encountered when young. This anger continues since I was still a Christian, because of bad attitudes toward women generally, and in one case very bad behavior by a youth leader toward me personally. I think that was the first true challenge to my belief system as a teenager actually.[9] I would have great difficulty affiliating myself in any way with the historic, culture- and soul-destroying practices and institutions that have been and continue to be imposed by Christian people on non-Christian [native] people . . . The impacts of missionization are repugnant to me. I also feel that I was not given the whole truth about the Christian "legacy" until I began studying it in university, and that makes me somewhat angry as well. What other institution asks us to buy in, in some cases be born in, and "details to follow"? (Former Believer 37)

---

8. Some church folk might prefer to say that Former Believers only "professed to be Christians." I prefer to take them at their word, that they were Christians.

9. Sadly, this kind of disillusionment with an authority figure is not uncommonly the catalyst from James Fowler's Stage Three to Stage Four.

I feel somewhat angry that I believed in Christianity in the first place. I feel to some extent that this was a wasted time, and am embarrassed by it. (Former Believer 31)

My Mom said that there was a movie once where a priest loses his faith and shows up at another church and shouts out questions from the back row. And all of the really TOUGH questions too. That's what I feel like doing a lot. (Former Believer 24)

Relief

Three feel a strong sense of relief at having left Christian faith:

No more pressure to get up and pretend every Sunday. (Former Believer 32)

I'm relieved that I don't feel guilt in the way I used to. (Former Believer 31)

Not having to answer for past mistakes and justify them to the "good Christian folk". (Former Believer 36)

Sadness

Only one person checks the box indicating a strong sense of sadness, but two people sound wistful at what has been lost:

There is a part of me that misses the community and shared values of a church congregation. This may seem incongruous with a lack of faith, but community values that are found in church are often more to do with the community values than that of a given religious outlook. (Former Believer 29)

I feel sad that I don't have that security anymore, nor that community. I always hope to find another community like that, that isn't based on Christianity, but it's not the same. (Former Believer 23)

Guilt and Amusement

Perhaps surprisingly, there is almost no residual guilt attached to the memory of leaving Christian faith. One woman, however, finds that others try to lay guilt on her:

> My parents and their "Christian friends." They preach love and yet look scornfully on a single mom. (Former Believer 36)

One other person says,

> "I feel amused" (Former Believer 32).

LOOKING BACK

When given the opportunity to comment on the leaving experience, several Former Believers speak warmly of the time when they were Christians:

> I believe that Christianity has useful answers, values, accumulated wisdom etc. to offer to people. I believe it was an enrichment to my youth to have been involved with the Church. (Former Believer 37)

> Though I was aware of negative Christian role models, these did not discount the good ones I was also aware of. (Former Believer 37)

> It was an excellent way for me to grow up, and feel supported. I have fond memories, and have taken values, morals and lessons with me through life. (Former Believer 29)

> Being a Christian at camp was easy, fun, powerful and peaceful. No matter how hard I tried to stay that way, all the feelings left when I returned home "to the real world". (Former Believer 26)

> I think Christianity is only one interpretation, and while it's totally beautiful and useful in its pure form, it's too often distorted. (Former Believer 23)

Christianity is too restrictive—though this isn't to say that I didn't relish the freedom of Christ and the freedom and security of the Christian community and life guidelines. (Former Believer 23)

The language here is strong and warm: "an enrichment to my youth", good role models, fond memories, "fun, powerful and peaceful," "totally useful and beautiful," "freedom in Christ." For those in church leadership, it is sobering to know that although these people made such a promising start in Christian faith and life, the counter-influences were so much stronger than all the church could offer.

THE PRESENT SPIRITUALITY OF FORMER BELIEVERS

Only two Former Believers now consider themselves atheists. The others still have a personal form of spirituality, which usually includes belief in a God of some kind, but they are not willing to make dogmatic statements about their present faith. None has joined another religion, though one says, "I am looking for answers elsewhere at the moment."

Two have become atheists

One speaks of leaving Christian faith because of a "feeling that there is no God" (Former Believer 29). The second goes into more detail:

> I simply found that belief in God was not logical. It seems
> to me that such a belief has always been and will always
> be a crutch—a way in which people can ignore or not deal
> with serious situations that confront. It justifies inhuman-
> ity and obscures personal responsibility. I would like to be
> absolutely clear as to the way in which I designate myself. I
> do not consider myself to be Christian but I do not subscribe
> to any other religion either. If asked, I respond in a semi-
> serious manner by indicating that I am a reborn Atheist. Such
> a response often elicits a rather strange reaction in that many

112

people seem to think that Atheist is a bad word. I do not find that to be the case nor to think that Atheism is synonymous with absence of spirituality. (Former Believer 32)

Most consider themselves to be "spiritual"

Two Former Believers associate this spiritual sense with the natural world:

My view of how my personal spirituality is manifested is still very unclear. I do know it is stronger when I am living close to the natural world, which can be attributed to camp in part. It is also the reason I have chosen to live in the country for the past 3 years. (Former Believer 37)

I believe in a higher power, I sometimes pray . . . I do feel that spirituality is a vital part of whole-health. Church, Bible studies, prayer meetings and supportive friends all provide really necessary things in order to live a happy and healthy life. I just feel one can get this support and faith in other ways. (Former Believer 29)

I believe that good things come to good people, and the Golden Rule. I believe that there is a higher power and that we all have an angel watching out for us. It's a peaceful image. (Former Believer 26)

I believe that we are caretakers of this earth, not that this earth is, or should be, our personal playground. I am closest to God in nature, I would rather go to listen to God beside a gurgling brook then in a regimental setting like a church. I think that God and I have an understanding. I do my best to protect his world, and my fellow man and he gives me what I need; shelter, food, a good job, and peace at the end of the day. (Former Believer XX)

Many are agnostic

Only one actually calls herself an "agnostic," but most Former Believers have come to what is basically an agnostic point-of-view: that human beings cannot know very much about "ultimate reality" and that the dogmatic certainty they experienced among Christians is not justified. Seven make such observations:

> I accept that we humans cannot and should not attempt to explain all that happens in this "world" as we don't know and are just guessing. We are too arrogant to accept that we don't know and can't say that we can't explain it. (Former Believer 38)

> I cannot describe my relation to spirituality except that I take a long time now to determine what and who is true and has spiritual value. (Former Believer 37)

> I feel as though I am spiritual because I feel as though there will always be things which are beyond the comprehension of any human being . . . Any system of belief, even philosophical, requires faith—a leap. (Former Believer 32)

> Religion is a basis in society that has been created by humans in an attempt to understand the beginnings of the earth. I feel that there is no difference between religions except a different human attempt to describe the unknown. (Former Believer 23)

> I'd say I'm an agnostic. I like to learn about different spiritual perspectives and maybe I'm just a humanist, and an anarchist a bit. (Former Believer 23)

> I still believe that there is a God . . . I believe that there are questions that can't be answered with pat quotes from the Bible. (Former Believer XX)

Once more, I am saddened that these people did not meet Christians who could help them make the transition to a more adult Christian faith. Many Christians are clear about what they believe, but at the same time know perfectly well that they do not have all the answers. This was spelled out long ago in the Bible:

The secret things belong to the LORD our God, but the revealed things belong to us and our children forever, to observe all the words of this law.[10]

When Christians fail to distinguish between the "secret" (about which we should be cheerfully agnostic) and the "revealed" (where we can be clear and firm, though humble), they become dogmatic where it is not appropriate. And young people in particular are put off by the rigid religion which results.

In this, I agree with Bishop John Robinson, who said:

Christ remains for the Christian absolutely central . . . Be free to admit that you are a Christian agnostic, that is a *Christian* who does not *know* a great deal . . . The centre for the Christian is firm: the edges and the ends are gloriously and liberatingly open.[11]

I asked these Former Believers whether they can envision any circumstances under which they would want to be Christians again. Not surprisingly, nine of them simply say No, they would never come back. Three give no answer. Two say they might return one day. One of these makes no comment. The second says:

I felt a bit indoctrinated as a kid and was very conscious of not wanting to make up my mind immaturely. Maybe this was rationalization, I don't know. I always thought that accepting Christ was a very adult thing that shouldn't be taken lightly . . . like voting maybe, that we only trust those who are over 18. (Former Believer 24)

This is maybe not such a bad idea, but some youth pastors might have to rethink much of their ministry.

---

10. Deuteronomy 29:29

11. John A. T. Robinson, *But That I Can't Believe!* (London: Fontana Books, 1967), 127.

MIGHT THINGS HAVE BEEN DIFFERENT?

I especially appreciate the fourteen people who filled out the Former Believers survey. For them it meant revisiting issues that have been closed, in some cases for years, and talking about events which were painful. By letting their voice be heard, I am quite sure they have spoken for many others who have in fact left Christian faith but did not reply to the survey.

The stories of this group are not easy for Christians to hear, but they need to be heard. Obviously there is a strong element of personal choice about the move these people have made away from faith. Even if the church had behaved perfectly, some would have wanted to leave.

But I find I am left with a certain wistfulness. After all, the Former Believers give us at least two clues as to what might have helped them on their journey. First, their answers suggest that more tolerance of questioning is needed from Christian leaders. This might be accomplished by offering a range of answers rather than single "right" answers to difficult and complex questions—such as the exclusive claims of Christianity in relation to other religious traditions. Second, if mature Christians had been able to come alongside as mentors and help these young believers navigate the complexities of arriving at an adult faith, I cannot help thinking that things might have been different.

These simple recommendations do not seem to be asking a great deal of mature believers.

As a leader, however, I have to be careful not just to point the finger at others. I find I ask myself, Did I miss the clues? Was I so quick to speak that I failed to listen carefully enough? Should I have been less busy and spent more time with someone? My guess is that anyone with pastoral instincts will ask those same questions. One respondent, a Loyal Believer, says, "I feel guilty, like perhaps if I had been a better friend they wouldn't have left." Such reflections make us uneasy.

Ultimately, I realize, people choose their own road, as God gives us freedom to do. And we are ultimately answerable to God for the choices we make. My hope (of course) is that in time that road might lead Former Believers back to faith—not the form of faith they left, but (as others have found) a deeper, more adult faith.[12]

Even if it never happens, however, I would like to hope at the very least that relationships between Former Believers and present believers might come about which are unpressured and friendly, and lead to mutual understanding. That does not seem too much to hope for.

---

12. Many have described just such a journey, including C.S.Lewis in *Surprised by Joy.*

6

OFF-ROAD ADVENTURES

Why Do Absent Believers Still Believe?

Colin did not grow up in church, but as a teenager, a friend invited him to a lively youth group, where after six months Colin had an evangelical conversion. Working at camp in the summers was the spiritual highlight of Colin's year, but it was always difficult going home to a family who did not sympathise with his faith. His Christian friends at university and the lively student church were the chief sources of spiritual nurture. After graduation, he went on to grad school in a different city, and got more involved in his local church where he tried to use his gifts of leadership. Within a couple of years, however, he was disillusioned with his church involvement. The preaching seemed to him simplistic, particularly compared with the challenges of his academic work, and there were few people his own age there. After a year or so, he simply stopped going. A fellow grad student invited him to work on a Habitat for Humanity team, and there he found fellowship and a worthwhile form of service, often with other "dechurched" Christians. He is still very clear about the fact that he is a Christian, and, under the right circumstances, he knows he could be persuaded to try church again—maybe when he gets his first job or if he finds a Christian woman he wants to marry.

So far, we have heard from many people who have persisted in faith and church, and those who have given up both faith and church.

Chapters 4 and 5 uncovered some of the reasons Loyal Believers carry on in their faith. Their answers included their relationship with God, their community (friends, family, camp, marriage), and a growth in the way they understand their faith.

Then in Chapter 6 we heard from people who have left church and faith. These Former Believers have been hurt by the church and disillusioned with the church. In particular, they could not live with what they understood to be the exclusive claims of Christianity.

There is still some mystery about the fact that many of the things the Former Believers complain about are similar to those mentioned by the Loyal Believers: why did the difficulties cause one group to give up, but not the other? Relationships seem to be one important key: relationships with God, with mentors and friends, and (to a lesser extent) with family.

The plot thickens, however, when we look at what was said by the second largest group: the Absent Believers—57 of them, making up 17% of the total responses. In many cases, they have experienced the same kind of problems described by both Loyal Believers and Former Believers. In the case of these Absent Believers, however, those experiences have driven them from the church (unlike the Loyal Believers) but not from faith (unlike the Former Believers). This is a group few other researchers have talked to, and yet they make up a distinct cohort, quite different from the others. So who are these people, and what makes them distinctive?

WHY DO ABSENT BELIEVERS CONTINUE TO CALL THEMSELVES CHRISTIANS?

I find that the first question I want to ask is: if you have dropped out of church, why would you bother to continue calling yourself a

Figure 11: Reasons for Staying Christian:
A comparison of Absent Believers and Loyal Believers
(proportion indicating "Important" or "Very important")

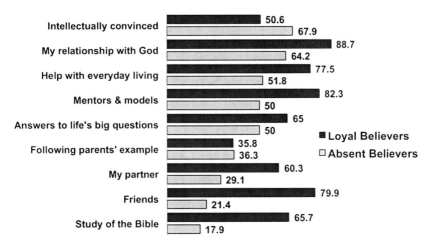

Christian? Would it not be simpler to stop using the word? Certainly, it might be easier, but for these people, there are important reasons they still think of themselves as committed Christians: their faith is much more than "nominal." There are also strong reasons they are not currently involved in church, and, if life is complicated as a result, they are prepared to live with that.

The reasons Absent Believers still call themselves Christians are markedly different from those of Loyal Believers. (The comparison may be seen in Figure 11.)

These are some of the most noticeable differences:

- The number one reason Absent Believers continue to believe is because they are intellectually convinced that Christianity is true. Intellectual satisfaction does not rate as highly for Loyal Believers, who rate it only ninth in importance.

- For Absent Believers, their "relationship with God" is still significant (64.2%), almost as important as their intellectual convictions, but still nothing like as important as it is for Loyal Believers (89%).
- Other relationships are less of an influence in helping Absent Believers stay Christians, whether mentors and models (50% compared with 82.3%), friends (29.1% compared with 80.9%), or a partner (29.1% compared with 60.3%). The only relationship which the two groups rate the same is their parents (36.3% compared with 35.8%).

My guess is that intellectual convictions have taken on more significance for keeping Absent Believers in the faith because Christian relationships have been missing for one reason or another. Conversely, for Loyal Believers strong relationships have meant it was less pressing to worry about intellectual issues of faith.

The comments of Absent Believers add colour to these statistics. They do not comment on the importance of their intellectual convictions, but they do have a lot to say about:

A relationship with God

Two-thirds of Absent Believers say they continue to call themselves Christians because of their relationship with God. The church may have failed them, they may have lost touch with friends, but there is still something about the reality of God in their lives that they cannot and will not deny.[1]

Fourteen Absent Believers write in comments about this. They say things like:

> I have been married 2.5 years and my wife and I, though only tenuously involved in a Church, both want to grow in our

---

1. Cf. In the UK similarly, "[m]any who had lost their faith in the church had not lost their faith in God" (Francis and Richter, 97).

personal relationship with God—and that is at the center of it all for me right now. (Absent Believer 35, United to Presbyterian)

I am still feeling the grace of God in my life. My faith flows from this specific point. (Absent Believer 32, XX)

[I am still a Christian because of] God always being there. (Absent Believer 29, Anglican)

For some people, I suspect that this kind of "relationship with God" outside of a church could have dissolved into a no-name brand of theism rather than a specifically Christian faith, but, for some at least, this is not the case. The "God" to whom they relate still has a Christian face:

I call myself a Christian because . . . the messages that the Bible delivers are the foundation of my core being. (Absent Believer 30, Presbyterian)

I still consider myself to be a Christian because I continue to believe that God is real and that Jesus died for our sins. (Absent Believer 27, Baptist)

I feel relieved that no matter what mistakes, what errors I make, and no matter how far I stray, well, God keeps up his end of the bargain no matter what. It's me that has to come back to his table—and he'll never give away my seat. I still call myself a Christian, so it's not really very far to look back. The Big J is still the man. Always was, always will be.☺[2] (Absent Believer 23, Christian and Missionary Alliance)

God is always there; Jesus died for my sins; God will never give away my seat. This is the kind of comment Absent Believers write in about their links with God. No wonder they will not give up the "Christian" label.

I notice too that these people have not retreated into a private kind of faith. Community still shows up in their comments, though

2. The smiley face was in the original, and I thought I should keep it.

not as "organized church": family and friends still figure largely in their comments.

The influence of family

As with Loyal Believers, Absent Believers speak warmly of their families and "the influence of my parents." Indeed, although it is not a statistically significant difference, they rate the effect of their families on their faith 4% higher than do Loyal Believers. What is significant is that for Absent Believers their family's influence is the sixth strongest influence, whereas for Loyal Believers it is thirteenth. Absent Believers say things like this:

> The family environment that I was brought up in. My Mom and Dad brought me up going to Church every Sunday . . . I have great talks with my parents, and they are the biggest encouragement in my life. (Absent Believer 34, Baptist)

> My inner strength was developed by my parents. (Absent Believer 30, United)

Often, Absent Believers link their relationship to their upbringing and their relationship with God in the same sentence. Twenty-four Loyal Believers also write about the influence of their upbringing on their faith, but I could not help noticing that what they say about personal faith is usually separate from what they say about family influence. Absent Believers, however, make statements like this:

> I was born into an Irish Catholic family, and draw strength [from] and identify with the cultural and political aspects of that religious heritage . . . [But] My embrace of Christianity is not simply because I was born into it, I did choose to follow Christian tenets as a young person. (Absent Believer 23, Catholic)

> I still call myself a Christian because . . . I continue to believe in the existence of a benevolent God and in the truth and beauty of Christ. I'm not sure this is much of a "choice" per se. I

couldn't all of a sudden choose not to believe. (Absent Believer 23, United)

I call myself a Christian because my roots are those of Christianity, the messages that the Bible delivers are the foundation of my core being . . . The reason why I call myself a Christian is not simply because of the influence of others, but [because of] how Christianity has influenced me. (Absent Believer 30, Presbyterian)

There is obviously an element of "cultural faith" here—people call themselves Christian because that is the culture in which they grew up. To traditional evangelicals, this might be seen as a weakness, indicating that someone has not made their family faith their own (as some people put it, "God has no grandchildren"). However, faith is usually the result of both environment and personal choice. Even the idea that a personal decision must be made is stressed in a particular kind of culture.

Nevertheless it may be the case that, for this group, at the moment anyway, their family background provides the same kind of impetus for faith that a church community gives to Loyal Believers. The question in my mind is how long that cultural capital can last before it runs out, unless it is "topped up" by a faith community in the present.

It is interesting that three Absent Believers specifically mention the influence of their mothers[3]:

My mom who died eight years ago . . . a woman of strong faith and I always look to her example. (Absent Believer 35, United to Presbyterian)

---

3. Another researcher, Kirk Hadaway, noticed that "An important correlate of growth in 'mature faith' among youth is whether or not they have talked about God recently with their mothers." Hadaway, 95. Hadaway and Roof also comment on the significance of a mother's faith: "If parents are regular attenders (especially mothers), apostasy is quite low." Bromley, 41.

My absolute belief in God and people like my Mom and others at my church who are excellent models affirm my belief in Christianity and its truth. (Absent Believer 25, Baptist)

My mother is a very strong Christian . . . Having a role model like that helped me not to give up on God when I didn't feel close to or understand God . . . I have a Grandfather who is VERY Christian who had faith in me when no one else did, and that helped me have faith in God. (Absent Believer 22, Anglican)

For what it is worth, although twenty-four Loyal Believers write comments about the influence of their parents, not one singles out the influence of their mother in this way. Though it is an over-simplification, there would seem to be some truth in saying that people will stay in faith because of their mothers, but it takes the faith of both parents to keep them in church.

Why do Absent Believers see their families as more influential than Loyal Believers do? One reason might be that other factors which maintain the faith of Loyal Believers are much weaker. Consider three factors I mentioned before:

(1) Though their relationship with God is strong, they do not rate it as highly as do Loyal Believers;

(2) They are less likely to have spiritual mentors They are less likely to regard spouses or partners as reasons for continuing in faith;

And (3) they have dramatically fewer Christian friends.

Partly as a result, some still have a question about what is inherited faith and what is personal faith, an issue Loyal Believers have generally resolved. In fact, one woman expresses her uncertainty quite poignantly:

Do I have this little thread of faith because of my upbringing in the Church? Or because it is genuine? Or because it is necessary? Or even because God's love is undeniable? I don't know. (Absent Believer 30, Presbyterian)

My guess is that the future in faith for Absent Believers depends on how they resolve that uncertainty. Will the influence of family, background and culture draw that person back to a strong personal faith based in a Christian community—or will they gradually evolve into Former Believers?

Influence of friends

What decides whether a person will stay a Loyal Believer or become an Absent Believer? The most dramatic difference is the influence of friends. To put it bluntly, the more strong, lasting friendships a young person has among Christians, the more likely they are to remain not only within the faith but also active in the church.

Three Absent Believers say it is friends who have helped them stay within the faith, saying things like:

> My closest friend is a friend I met . . . at Pioneer many years ago. She did keep in touch and has been a lifelong friend and confidante. (Absent Believer 32, United)

> The friendships I have made through Pioneer over the years as a camper and as staff have been significant (especially those in a mentor type role who have invested in my life). (Absent Believer 22, Catholic)

What I notice is missing among the comments of Absent Believers is the kind of comment made by Loyal Believers, that their friends explicitly encourage them and challenge them in their faith. Only one Absent Believer makes a comment even slightly of this kind:

> I do have contact . . . with some old friends who inspire me to continue striving in my Christian beliefs, though now less than ever in my life. (Absent Believer 35, United to Presbyterian)

It may be significant that two of the three who talk about friends say that these friends were made at camp. At least for someone over

30, this is half a lifetime ago! It suggests that they have not found other "spiritual friends" along the way.

One does say he wishes he had more Christian friends: "I have no close friends who are church-going Christians, although I wish I did." (Absent Believer 25, Baptist) Of course, to some extent this is a vicious circle: if I am not involved in church, I am less likely to have Christian friends, and if I lack Christian friends, it will weaken my interest in going to church where I might make Christian friends.

The importance of friends shows up at other points too. For instance, in the next chapter there is some evidence that it can be friends who help an Absent Believer make a fresh start in church life. And when someone is checking out a church to attend, one focus group member said she looks for "nice people who are (hopefully) my age and that I have something in common with"—in other words, people with whom there is the potential for friendship.

Christian activities outside of church

I was curious to know whether, since Absent Believers have given up on formal church, they were involved in any "church substitute" activities, such as a small group of like-minded Absent Believers, or a social action program. My guess was that Absent Believers might well be meeting with others who think as they do, and that they might be involved in some activity where they had found churches lacking.

The question asked whether they are "involved in Christian activities other than church", such as a small group, camp activities, or social outreach programs. They were then asked whether this is a regular commitment, and if so, how often they are involved, and for how long they have been involved. Finally, they were asked whether they find this activity "more spiritually satisfying than church" and whether some of those they meet in the course of this activity are also Christians who are not active in church.

Their responses show that, while Absent Believers may not be involved in church, nineteen out of the fifty-six (one-third) are

Figure 12: Church-like Activities of Absent Believers (proportion indicating involvement)

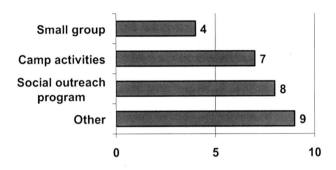

active in different activities that express and nurture their faith. Out of those nineteen, thirteen say this is "more satisfying than church" and ten say they have found other Absent Believers involved in these activities. (See Figure 12.) Most of the comments are about social outreach activities and small groups.[4]

Social outreach activities

Eight Absent Believers talk about being involved in social outreach activities, from Habitat for Humanity to street ministry. Typical is a 32-year-old Presbyterian who has been involved monthly with other Absent Believers in a social outreach program for the past three years, and finds this more satisfying than church. Here are some other comments:

---

4. Most who indicate "Other" do not say what the activity is, but one is in an Alpha program, and another is taking "motivation and leadership courses." Both of these are in their 30's.

I've volunteered for Habitat for Humanity [irregularly for the past two years]: my motivation to do volunteer work stems from guilt that I lead a very selfish life (I don't have a spouse or children even therefore my life seems to center around my own interests) and a belief that the answers to the big life questions lie in action. (Absent Believer 30, Presbyterian)

[I work at a] drop in center for the homeless. (Absent Believer 29, Anglican)

I have participated in activities in the past like a mission working with street people, making meals for street people at Evergreen and Sanctuary in Toronto, and participating in social justice efforts, such as joining peace marches against the war in Iraq. (Absent Believer 23, Catholic)

I am involved with many organizations such as Amnesty International, the United Nations, various university groups and a shelter for women experiencing domestic abuse. Although these groups are not specifically Christian, I certainly believe that they carry out work that is pleasing to God, and have this in mind when I participate. (Absent Believer 23, United)

These are demanding commitments, involving significant idealism and time. If the churches these people attended when they were teenagers had offered this kind of activity, maybe it would have been easier for them to stay within the church.

It is noticeable that these particular respondents are all from mainline church backgrounds, where social action is more taken for granted as an expression of Christian faith than it is in evangelical churches. My guess is that when Absent Believers from evangelical churches give up on church, they are less likely to move on to this kind of "church substitute" activity, but I do not have enough data to know that for certain.

Small group

Seven say they are involved in small groups with others who share their skepticism about church.

One, for example, has been enjoying "Social activities with Christian friends [who] share similar values" (Absent Believer 34, Baptist) weekly for the past fifteen years, and finds this "more satisfying than church." Another has been involved for over ten years in monthly "informal gatherings of friends who share the idea that faith is a long journey." He explains, "It is the idea that faith comes with a responsibility to recognize that we are interconnected and must attempt in our own way to speak out on issues that concern civil society and the religious life." (Absent Believer 32, XX)

I suspect that this kind of group is more common than anyone has yet researched. After all, they do not advertise, they do not go out to recruit new members (except occasionally on a one-to-one basis), and there is no reason an outsider would even know they exist. I believe that, for these people, such groups are a substitute for church. As one respondent says:

> I consider many of the [social concern] activities I participate in to be part of the "church in action," even if they are not formally connected to the organized church. (Absent Believer 23, United)

It is true that such groups often lack the mix of generations you find in a local congregation, they have no sacraments, and they lack any formal link to the broader church. But for people who participate in them, the benefits such as honesty and shared ideals makes it a worthwhile trade-off.[5]

Five of the respondents who are still in university mention small Christian groups on campus. One emphasizes that it is "definitely more spiritually satisfying than church" (Absent Believer 22, Catholic). However, a student small group like this, which is

---

5. Dave Tomlinson describes such a group in his book, *The Post-Evangelical* (London: Triangle, 1995). The group, known as "Holy Joe's" meets on Tuesday nights in the lounge of a bar in a south London pub. He believes that "tens of thousands of people continue to practise their faith privately [in this kind of way], whilst finding no real relevance for church in their lives." (12)

temporary by nature, is not the same as a group of people in their 30s, like the two mentioned above. And, of course, being involved in a student group does not mean someone has become an Absent Believer. As one student says:

> Haven't really ever dropped church, just never really got settled in a church community . . . and still involved in other Christian activities. (Absent Believer 22, Catholic)

Often when students graduate from university, and leave this kind of rich fellowship behind, they find it difficult to enter the world of "normal church," where such fellowship is often lacking. No wonder some settle for something like a small group outside the life of a local congregation. It would be interesting to know whether churches with an active small group program are more likely to hold the loyalty of young Christians. I suspect the answer would be yes.

FAITH . . . BUT NOT CHURCH

For Absent Believers faith, specifically Christian faith, is still an important reality. They are by no means Former Believers, and most do not see themselves moving in that direction. Nevertheless, they have dropped out of church, even though they often find "church substitutes" among friends and social activities.

So what was it that caused them to leave church in the first place? And can they imagine themselves moving back into church life at some point? What would it make to turn an Absent Believer into a Loyal Believer? The next chapter will consider these questions.

7

UNDERSTANDING THE OFF-RAMPS

Why Do Absent Believers Leave Church?

If you have read this far, it will not come as a surprise to know that Absent Believers left church life because of problems with the church. (See Figure 13.) Just over half (51.9%) speak of disillusionment with the church; 48.2% say they cannot find "a church they like"; 40.7% complain of hypocrisy; 22.3% complain of the high expectations of church life[1]; and 17% say church was simply irrelevant. There are 13 "write-in" responses on this topic. The litany of complaints is familiar: oppressive leadership, lifestyle restrictions, legalism, and guilt-trips.

Some might ask, Aren't they exaggerating? Certainly there will be another side to many of these stories. If we could interview all the parties involved, we would get a more balanced impression of what went wrong. Yet if only 50% of these stories were found to be accurate, they are still deeply saddening. In any case, even if some

---

1. This should not be confused with the normal demands of Christian discipleship.

Figure 13: What caused Absent Believers to leave?
Proportion indicating "Important" or "Very important"

Disillusionment with church	51.9
Not finding a church I liked	48.2
Hypocrisy in church	40.7
Ethical disagreement with church	30.8
Not settled down	28
Unanswered theological questions	22.3
Expectations of church involvement	22.3
Lifestyle pressure	22.2
Work pressure left no time	20.4
Finding church irrelevant	17
Finding an unbelieving partner	11.1
God let me down	9.5
A catastrophe	5.7
Need to be independent of parents	1.9
Negative peer pressure	1.8

accounts might be "explained away," that would be a bit like trying to avoid individual rocks in an avalanche. Certainly you could work out how to avoid some, but avalanches do not come rock by rock: they are simply overwhelming.[2] Here is a selection of the comments. See what you think.

> I shut down during that time and became disillusioned with those who judged me. My divorce was the catalyst to my decline in church attendance. (Absent Believer 31, Christian Reformed)

> Being lied to by religious mentors, being shunned rather than accepted for mistakes that I made, being belittled by senior church leaders because of my youth. People seem to have an annoying habit of tearing apart in stupidity what was built to restore and bring hope. (Absent Believer 30, Presbyterian)

---

2. This is a paraphrase of an analogy from B. B. Warfield's *The Inspiration and Authority of the Bible* (London, 1959), 119-120.

My issues do not have a lot to do with Christianity as a religion or a life-style; it has to do with individuals running organized groups or a church who misuse their power to influence others and their lives. (Absent Believer 28, Baptist)

I constantly felt guilty if I did not do all that was expected of me: reading the Bible every day, witnessing to others, going to Bible study. Being involved in the church was so much work that it took away from my relationship with God. (Absent Believer 27, Baptist)

Apparently Jesus would never have befriended or hung out with the poor, the desolate, gays, anybody not middle class. The thing that irks me most is the WWJD ["What Would Jesus Do?"] buttons and stickers, which, in my experience, have been worn by some of the least tolerant, least loving people. (Absent Believer 27, Anglican)

The rather constant internal mental searches of Christians ("Am I doing this for the 'right' reasons?" "Am I following God's will?" etc.) were frightening for me since I was positive that I wasn't going to like what I found in me. As much as I'm still struggling with the meaning of Christianity and how it applies to me now, I do miss it. (Absent Believer 26, Congregationalist)

I have issues with the corporatist church and its inflexibility and [lack of] understanding, and the tendency of other Christians to judge rather than support. (Absent Believer 25, United)

I am sad that I don't have a Christian community and that Christians became the enemy in a time when I needed Christian love most. (Absent Believer 22, Anglican)

Being judged, the misuse of power, guilt, too much introspection, inflexibility, not loving when love was needed. Frankly, the list is depressing. In some ways, the saddest is the comment that church "took away from my relationship with God," when one critical function of church is to enable and nurture a relationship with God. Ironically, for many of these people, leaving church was necessary for their spiritual survival. Churches should not treat anybody this way, but it is particularly tragic that these things happened to young Christian leaders whose potential influence on the future of the church we may have irrevocably lost.

Lifestyle issues

For Absent Believers, almost one-third (30.8%) agreed strongly that they "disagreed with various ethical beliefs in the church." Some of the problems concern what might be called cultural issues, such as alcohol consumption, while others are more "hard-core" ethical questions.

Three Baptists, one Anglican and one United mention cultural issues. The following is typical:

> I found the church too critical/ controlling . . . I believe in having a balanced lifestyle and have found Christians to be very hypocritical towards lifestyle decisions. I enjoy a glass of wine with dinner—but some Christians would consider this wrong etc. (Absent Believer 34, Baptist)

One person, however, made the liberating discovery that not all Christians view such things the same way by the simple expedient of crossing the Atlantic into a different church culture:

> The culture of Britain rang true with me, and I was comfortable with it. I liked the fact that one local minister invited a few of us down to the pub, we all drank one pint of beer, and I didn't feel like a total traitor to my faith . . . [I]n Europe and the UK, I was exposed to people who . . . were committed Christians, and who made me feel good about my faith, rather than bad, as my church in Canada had done. (Absent Believer 25, Baptist)

Five make statements about finding themselves to the "left" of their churches in terms of more significant ethical issues. One Baptist of 25 is typical in writing, "Various churches that I have 'tried' have seemed conservative in their ethical stances on various issues." Here is one of the strongest statements (it is interesting that drinking is included in the list of what many would consider more significant ethical issues):

> I cannot agree to never have a drink socially, to not have worldly rather than Godly opinions about certain things, to treat gays as though they aren't just like me, to believe that born-again Christians never have abortions and feel it was the right decision. In spite of my love for God and my desire to regain my closeness to him, I just don't seem to belong to the "club." I know God understands this about me, He does, but the Christians I meet and most admire don't. I am an outcast for them, a horrible person. (Absent Believer 38, Baptist)

Other write-in comments talk about sexism in the church, lack of interest in social issues, racism (not least in attitudes towards native Canadians), too many denominations, gossip, and a controlling leadership style.[3]

Meeting "non-Christians" of Christian character outside "the bubble"

Several Absent Believers were surprised and confused by meeting people who do not claim to be Christians but who demonstrate integrity and compassion—sometimes more than those who do claim to be Christians:

> In my life experience, persons with whom I associate do not subscribe to any particular religion. These are people who show behaviors that are most like Jesus. Acceptance, compassion, non-judgmental, reaching out to embrace others who are from many walks of life. People within the churches I have attended showed many of the opposite behaviors. (Absent Believer 30, Christian Reformed)

---

3. One person writes, "I lost interest at Bible College." It is a unique and intriguing comment, but no more is said.

I feel saddened by the fact that my non-Christian friends (for the most part) have been more supportive and less judgmental than my Christian ones. It hurts to see the hypocrisy. (Absent Believer 24, Associated Gospel Churches)

I started moving away from the kind of faith and Christian life/ activities I was shown at Pioneer Camp when I met more people from a diverse array of backgrounds and faiths. I saw God so clearly in these people, it really made me question what I had been told (particularly at Pioneer) about Christianity being the only right way, and the necessity of spending a very large part of my time with other people who profess Christian faith. (Absent Believer 23, United)

The combination of finding good people outside the church and sin inside the church seems to come as a surprise to people across the denominations.[4] My guess is that parents and youth pastors, concerned for the well-being of their young people, have stressed the dangers of "the world" outside the church more than the reality of God at work in "the world." Certainly there are times when it is important to stress "the dangers of the world"—but if this is all churches teach, it hardly prepares young Christians to move out to live and work in that same world.

One Absent Believer speaks passionately to this issue:

---

4. Loyal Believers encountered the same challenge, though it did not cause them to leave church or faith. One says, "There are many non-Christians I know whom I would consider to be more spiritually aware than some Christians I know." (Loyal Believer 32, Anglican to United) Another writes: "I seem to have encountered so many individuals outside of the Christian faith who reflect more of Christ's character than Christians themselves." (Loyal Believer 23, Presbyterian to non-denominational) A third says: "Working at a campus radio station, I have come across a diverse group of people, which has stretched my rather narrow view of how God works with people." (Loyal Believer 30, Methodist to Catholic). In her case, however, this has strengthened her faith so that she says, as a result, "I participate [in church] with greater awareness."

My MOST screwed up friends are those who were sequestered in church/Christian families all their lives. It fosters an insecurity and "us against them" mentality, stemming from the repeated belief that the outside or "secular" world is all evil. Yes, yes, I know about that whole "in the world but not of the world" stuff, but people lose ANY ability to relate to everyday folks. Whenever I travel to churches, I see that glazed-over look of the lifelong Christian. Doesn't have to be that way. Less fear and more friendliness is what Christians should have. (Absent Believer 30, Anglican)

This problem is labeled by a number of respondents as the Christian "bubble." What they refer to is that fact that a Christian young person's life can be largely taken up with church activities—youth group, church services, even sports teams and other "non-religious" activities—leaving little time for "normal" interaction with non-church folks. Here are three complaints about "the bubble", all from younger respondents—maybe because they have only recently realised the problems this has caused them:

I lived such a sheltered life, in a bubble, and it just got to a point where I wasn't sure that I liked the environment in the bubble anymore. (Absent Believer 24, Associated Gospel Church)

Perhaps there should be more emphasis on recognizing that we do not exist in a tidy Christian bubble—and if we do, we are not living very full lives. (Absent Believer 23 Catholic)

One urges church leaders:

Be a part of society and culture—church bubbles are easy to form and difficult to break. (Absent Believer 23, non-denominational)

I believe this is not just a problem of practice, but also of theology. I wonder particularly whether those who felt unprepared for life "outside the bubble" were taught about "common grace" in their churches.[5] This is the doctrine which explains that God gives good gifts to all humankind, whether or not they believe. Jesus summarises this idea in the Sermon on the Mount by saying, "God makes his sun rise on the evil and on the good, and sends rain on the righteous and on the unrighteous."[6] As a result, a believer should not be surprised that the Creator gives to all his creatures such blessings as generous hearts, strong marriages, rich friendships, and so on. When Christians encounter "non-Christians" who behave like Christ, they should simply be happy at the generosity of the Creator![7]

Moving to a new town

Living in a mobile society has a radical effect on people's church involvement. I have already referred to Reginald Bibby's observation that:

> Statistics Canada estimates that the average Canadian makes
> a residential move about once every five years . . . Residential
> movement is a major source of attrition for religious groups . . .
> Every time people move, about half of them will stop attending
> regularly.[8]

And, as he then adds, "the most residentially-mobile people in Canada are young adults." This is often a problem for Absent Believers, 28% of whom identify strongly with the statement, "I

---

5. The idea of "common grace" has been particularly discussed in Reformed churches. See, for example, Richard Mouw, *He Shines In all That's Fair: Culture and Common Grace* (Grand Rapids: Eerdmans 2001).

6. Matthew 5:45.

7. The Apostle Paul's evangelistic appeal at Lystra is not for people to repent of their sins, but for them to turn to God in gratitude for God's good gifts (Acts 15:8-18).

8. Bibby 1995, 78. Tony Lee points out that it would interesting to compare the faith retention rates of those who leave home to go to university with those who go to university while living at home. (Private communication.)

haven't lived long enough in one place to settle in a church." Six of them comment on this difficulty:

> I moved cities and never seemed to get re-connected with another church community. (Absent Believer 38, Baptist)

> Moved out of town and have not pursued a replacement church closer to me. (Absent Believer 29, Baptist)

For some, moving means driving further to a church they really like:

> Moved away—it's now a 45 minute drive to our church. We've never felt comfortable anywhere else we've attended. (Absent Believer 33, United)

Few people who drive to church drive more than twenty minutes. If a family like this does not find a new church in which they are "comfortable," the odds are that they will gradually stop attending altogether.

In some of these comments, there is a trace of wistfulness:

> My husband and I have moved several times in the last ten years and have not established ourselves in a church. However, I recognize that this could be a bit of a cop out. (Absent Believer 35, Baptist)

> It has been hard because I haven't been able to settle in one place for several years. Some day. (Absent Believer 35, United to Presbyterian)

Will they decide that it's time to stop "copping out"? Will the "some day" actually come? The next chapter suggests that some will return to church eventually—and why.

Suffering

Suffering does not seem to have been as big a challenge to the faith of Absent Believers (5.7%) as it is for Loyal Believers (12%).

The difference, of course, is that those "catastrophes" did not cause Loyal Believers to leave the church, whereas Absent Believers did. The statistical gap is not a huge one, but it does reinforce the impression that on the whole the problem of suffering is not a major reason that people leave faith and church.

Having said that, at the same time the five stories people tell are deeply poignant, and I want to honour their vulnerability by including their stories here:

> My own mental illness from which I prayed and begged to be delivered through years of unimaginable pain from the time I was about 23 until I was about 33. I was close to suicide, but finally found medication that worked for me which I continue to take and I am probably about the happiest and most successful I have ever been . . . except God continues to nag me about my lack of involvement in church and I become more and more concerned as my preschoolers begin school, wondering where and how they will find a faith that will withstand anything. Thankfully, God is not going to leave me be until I deal with this. (Absent Believer 28, Baptist)

> My father passed away when I was 18 of a terminal illness he suffered from for 2.5 years. (Absent Believer 26, Congregationalist)

A third simply states, "Suicide of two of my closest friends" (Absent Believer 22, United) and another writes, "Death of father." (Absent Believer XX, Orthodox)

Only one says explicitly that he left church because of a traumatic experience:

> After I went to university, I began to deal with my father's alcoholism and its effects, and sought the counsel of a Christian psychologist. But, at the same time, I was already disengaging myself from the church, because I believed at that time that no one there could truly understand how difficult my home life was while I was growing up, specifically in my teens. (Absent Believer 25, Baptist)

What is interesting, of course, was that though these traumas drove Absent Believers out of the church, they managed to hang on to their faith. Was the support of the church inadequate? Was the pain that Absent Believers felt they could not face people, even caring people? The questions are poignant.

A mixture of factors

We saw in a previous chapter that Loyal Believers normally stay in faith and church because of more than one influence. In the same way, most Absent Believers say it was a mixture of factors that pushed them away from church.[9] The following story makes clear how different elements—personal questioning, work schedule, lifestyle choices, feeling judged, and feeling inadequate as a Christian, all worked together:

> I was 27 years old, and was questioning life: Who am I? What am I doing? I moved out of my parents' house and lost my virginity within the day. Started seeking answers for unan-swered questions elsewhere . . . God did not have any answers at that time, although I still seek answers from him now . . . I left the Church, because work would not allow me to attend on a regular basis. I was starting to question going prior to work being a conflict because I didn't like being judged by those members at the church. There was nothing at church to get me out of bed and go. Sunday became a day of sleep. I left because of a lack of answers from the church and a feeling of being judged. Everybody at church pretended to have their life sorted out. I'm not perfect and will never be. I now know that those people at church were also not perfect. I left church in a huff, without looking back. (Absent Believer 30, United)

---

9. Cf. Francis and Richter: "It would be unusual to identify a church-leaver whose disengagement from church was related solely to one of the 15 themes of our typology and to none of the others" (303).

There is a lot in this comment. Maybe the saddest sentence is, "There was nothing at church to get me out of bed and go." Here is a person asking the sort of questions to which Christian spirituality claims to have significant answers, and needing the kind of loving support Christians are supposed to offer—but the experience of church served only to drive her away rather than draw her near. What would it take for this person to have an experience of church such that, when her life is in turmoil, she would say, "Heck, I know it's Sunday morning and I usually sleep in, but I'm going to get myself to church today because they may be the only ones who can help me"?

THE EXPERIENCE OF LEAVING

What was the experience of leaving the church community like for Absent Believers? The results are similar to those of Former Believers. Almost half of the Absent Believers (47.2%) say the process of leaving was an easy one, and nearly the same number (52.8%) say it was a gradual process. Seventeen give the age at which they "left": of those, fourteen say the change took place during their late high school or university years. This is typical of those who drop out of church across North America.

When they comment on the leaving process, some familiar themes recur—moving house, being hurt by church, going to university, the lifestyle of university, the loss of friends, and simply growing up and thinking for oneself:

> [Leaving took] About four months. I joined the Inter-Varsity group with two other friends from camp. Two of us began feeling unwelcome and under secret attack by the group because of our partying. (Absent Believer 27, United)

> Leaving the youth group was easy to do at the time because of my anger. Over time, the choice I made often felt painful and difficult. [I was] 19 and in first year university. [The process took] A few years—probably two years when I really realized

144

that I was not participating like I did when I was living at home. (Absent Believer 26, Congregationalist)

[How long did the process take?] About as long as it did to decide that my bed was a much nicer place Sunday mornings than a hard pew would be. (Absent Believer 24, United)

The experience of being a student, and various summers spent traveling around did not allow me to settle into one single church. I thus simply dropped out. (Absent Believer 23, Christian and Missionary Alliance)

I was still involved with my church when I returned home, but while at school, I drifted away from church life. A year later I was also no longer regularly involved with church when at home. (Absent Believer 23, United)

As soon as I was an adult my parents didn't pressure me to be involved in the church. I took advantage of my sudden freedom and slowly lost my connection with the church. (Absent Believer 23, United)

Church stopped having anything to do with my life. I wasn't getting anything from it (e.g. support, wisdom, encourage-ment), and it was a choice between Saturday nights and Sunday mornings. Saturday nights won. (Absent Believer 22, Anglican)

The process took a couple of years, as I gradually lost contact with some of my camp friends who were influential in my Christian activities. (Absent Believer 22, United)

Almost half (49.1%) say that nobody noticed what was happening to them. However, it is clear from a number of comments that families were often concerned:

Looking back it was very distressing for my family. [It was a] sad time spiritually for me. I moved out west and worked in the ski business full time. Sundays was a work day and church was not an option. (Absent Believer 34, Baptist)

145

I realize there is a limit to how far a youth worker can continue to be involved with members of their group once they move on to university. After all, a new generation of young people is coming along immediately, and demanding full attention. But there may be times when a visit, or a card, or an email, from a youth group leader or mentor, to a former member who is now at university, might help. Perhaps if this kind of leader could visit on a weekend, where they could check out a local church together, or meet up with Christians on campus for lunch, might mean some good Christian connections could be made in this new and challenging world.

WHERE ARE ABSENT BELIEVERS HEADING?

A number of comments made by Absent Believers suggest that they will make their way back to church one day. For example:

> I miss the closeness of a community of like-minded and caring people. (Absent Believer 38, Baptist)

> God continues to nag me about my lack of involvement in church. (Absent Believer 38, Baptist)

> In the past, church allowed me to work out certain questions I had in my life. Since those have been somewhat answered I don't feel the necessity of involvement at this point in my life. I feel that I may return at some point in my life. (Absent Believer 22, United)

They were asked, "If you can imagine anything that would cause you to want to return to church and/or Christian activities, what would it be?"

- Twenty-six (46%) say they would return if they found "a good church";
- Nineteen (34%) say settling down and the influence of a spouse or children would bring them back;
- and seven (12%) say the influence of a friend would be the trigger.

146

In other words, if the church is concerned about those who have drifted away, there are things it can do. In particular, the idea of a "good church" is something I will explore in chapter 9. "Good churches" are out there and, of course, there are steps a "mediocre church" can take to become a "good church"!

Meanwhile, let us look at what respondents say about these three areas which might draw them back: being settled, marriage and family, and friends:

Being more settled

Many Absent Believers say that they would want to come back to church once they begin to "settle down." For some, this means less mobility, presumably job-related. Thus, when asked what would cause them to return, they say things like:

> Having children. Being settled in one place. (Absent Believer 35, United to Presbyterian)

One person combines the need to be more "settled" with a fairly demanding list of requirements in a "good church":

> Being settled in one place for a substantial amount of time and finding a church that I felt was truly after God's best and not just going through the motions, one that is not about religion but about Christ, that isn't just about winning souls but about loving people. (Absent Believer 22, Catholic)

Most churchgoers, moving to a new neighbourhood, choose a house first, then maybe the schools, and only after that look round to see what churches happen to be within reach. One respondent, however, thinks finding "the right church" sufficiently important that he is willing to move in order to live nearer to the church. If church is that significant a part of one's life, why not? After all, when people have children, they look for a home in the area where there are "good schools." Another person says:

147

The church we do attend is a distance away but we attend whenever we can and plan to buy a home in the same city as the church. (Absent Believer 32, United)

Someone else is also prepared to move, but work will have to change too. He is thinking of:

Moving closer and having a different work schedule. (Absent Believer 33, United)

One Returned Believer spells out the corollary that having found "the right church" might be a reason for staying put: she so appreciates her church "that now I am loath to move to a new location because I can't take my church with me" (Returned Believer 26, Methodist to Baptist).

Behind the connection between church membership and settling down is the reality that church is a long-term commitment. It is not like visiting your favourite restaurant chain in an unfamiliar city, where, as long as the menu is the same, who serves you does not matter very much. It is more like registering in a school[10], where the assumption is that you are more than a passing visitor. While Western society remains as mobile as it is, this will always be a problem.

Spouse, children, family

Anyone who has looked into why people leave and return to churches will not be surprised that only 29.1% of Absent Believers are married, compared with more or less twice that number of Loyal and Returned Believers. Only 20% have children, compared with virtually double that number among Loyal and Returned Believers. (See Figures 14 and 15.) One sociologist speaks for many:

---

10. This helpful image of the church is explored in detail by Robert Brow in his 1981 book, *Go Make Learners* , now to be found on the web at http://www. brow.on.ca/Books/Learners/LearnersIntro.html.

[R]esearchers in recent years have agreed that many young adults "come back" to church life after a period of absence, generally returning when they enter adult roles, such as marriage, parenthood, home ownership, and (in the upper middle class) career commitment.[11]

Absent Believers would not be surprised by this either. A good number of them actively expect to return to church when they marry and/or have children.[12] Fourteen (a very high number) write about

Figure 14: Who is married?

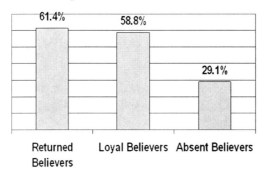

Returned Believers   Loyal Believers   Absent Believers

Figure 15: Who has children?

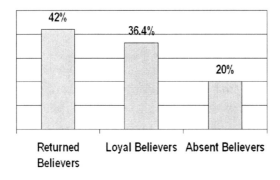

Returned Believers   Loyal Believers   Absent Believers

---

11. Hoge, Johnson and Luidens, 40.

12. Some who have already returned nevertheless chose to fill out the survey for Absent Believers. Perhaps they do not yet feel rooted enough to say that they are actually "involved" in church.

this. When they were asked under what circumstances they might consider returning to church, they said things like:

> If I have children, I would introduce them to the church and incorporate Christianity into our lives. (Absent Believer 32, Presbyterian)

> It might start with finding a nice Christian woman to help me want to be involved. I pretty much avoid Christian women because I have felt judged by them for having been divorced. (Absent Believer 31, Christian Reformed)

> Having a family of my own. (Absent Believer 29, non-denominational)

> My wife and eventually children. (Absent Believer 28, Associated Gospel Church)

> Marriage and (soon) a family have brought me to the point that I will settle into a church. (Absent Believer 28, Associated Gospel Church)

One Returned Believer makes explicit the connection between church and having children in his own life:

> I find that my wife and I have renewed interest in the growth of our faith since the birth of our first child. We definitely drifted away from regular church attendance in the first few years of our marriage. (Returned Believer 32, Catholic)

Some say openly that the reason they want to come back is not nostalgia for what they experienced in their childhood, nor even a desire to grow their faith in a church again, but simply that they want their children to have Christian instruction:

> Children—wanting them to learn about Christ in a positive environment. (Absent Believer 32, Presbyterian)

> I can imagine returning to church when I have children. I believe it is a good basis for learning morals, right and wrong,

and to be reassured of the love of God. (Absent Believer 30, Christian Reformed)

Having children—I would want them to be exposed to Christianity and church life so that they can make up their own mind. (Absent Believer 27, Baptist)

Getting married and having children. I want my children to be exposed to the teachings of Christianity and to grow up in a religious household. (Absent Believer 27, United)

I am curious to know what the experience of returning "for the sake of the children" will be like.[13] What about the problems that drove people away from church in the first place? In many cases those difficulties will not have gone away. What will happen to the faith that has been expressed either privately or in a non-church group setting? How will it change, if at all? Will that be difficult?

And a practical question: can church leaders expect that "Returnees" will be as involved in church as they were before? Other research, in both the US and Britain, suggests that the answer is no.[14] In Chapter 8, we will look in more depth at Returned Believers, and learn how they get involved in church life again. The answer, for these people anyway, is somewhat different.

---

13. Dr. Graham Room, a sociologist at Bath University in the UK, suggests that perhaps returning to church "enables parents to re-try their church experience to some extent vicariously through their children" (Personal correspondence).

14. Roof and Johnson say that that in the US "Returnees . . . are somewhat less likely to consider themselves religious, to believe in God, to hold church membership, to view the congregation as important, to attend regular services, to have a strong denominational identity, and to feel closer to others of the same religion than to other people." David A. Roozen and C. Kirk Hadaway (eds.) *Church and Denominational Growth: What does (and does not) cause Growth and Decline* (Nashville: Abingdon Press, 1993), 205. Gibbs and Brierley found a similar phenomenon in the UK and Australia. Gibbs, 286.

Friends

The influence of friends is just about as important in encouraging Absent Believers to come back to church as it was for Loyal Believers to stay in the faith. Several Absent Believers say they would go back to church if they had a friend to go with:

> If I had many friends who attended a particular Church, I would be more inclined to increase my attendance at Church. (Absent Believer 30, Anglican)

> Close friendship with someone who was a believer and went to a church that I felt was a good fit for me. (Absent Believer 27, Baptist)

> If I was able to make friends with someone who was a peer, I would be very interested in going to church with them. (Absent Believer 25, Baptist)

> Having someone to go to church with me. (Absent Believer XX, Orthodox)

> If there was a church close to my home that felt right to me I would go. Also it would be nice to have someone to go with. (Absent Believer XX, XX)

Some might think, Why don't they just get their act together and go to the nearest church? Yet regular churchgoers have long forgotten just how difficult it is to go to church for the first time, even for people who were once church members. Reg Bibby quotes one minister who decided to go to a different church on his Sunday off. He writes:

> As the worship hour drew nearer, I found my anxiety level rising . . . As I drove into the parking lot, my anxiety level rose even higher! I didn't know what was expected of me or what they actually do. As I entered the building, I actually found

myself perspiring . . . It's pretty tough to do it alone. Who needs all that anxiety on the day of rest?[15]

If this is true for a pastor in active ministry, how much moreso for someone who has been away for some time, and was perhaps badly hurt on the previous occasion? Thus when an Absent Believer says they find it difficult to come back, they deserve our sympathy:

In spite of my love for God and my desire to regain my closeness to him, I just don't seem to belong to the "club." I know God understands this about me—he does—but the Christians I meet and most admire don't. I am an outcast for them, a horrible person. (Absent Believer 38, Baptist)

I have no motivation to wake up early on a Sunday morning and attend Church alone. It's difficult to feel comfortable when you don't know a single person in the congregation. (Absent Believer 27, United)

Each church has its own culture, its own way of doing things; relationships are familiar and fairly set; in most churches a newcomer stands out; and most churches, however sincere, feel awkward and fumbling when trying to welcome a new person. The whole experience can be deeply embarrassing, and requires great will power.

No, the instinct that "I would go to church if I had a friend to go with" is perfectly legitimate. The question is really: where are the friends? Many admit they have drifted away from friends who do go to church and who might invite them. Perhaps Loyal Believers need to think whether there are Absent Believers whom they could invite and for whom they could be that friend.

BEGINNING THE RETURN

A few Absent Believers are already beginning to explore new church and faith options, even though in some cases it is tentative:

---

15. Bibby 1995, 52.

I am not currently involved in Christian activities; however, I am seeking a Christian community. (Absent Believer 35, Baptist)

I still call myself a Christian and never stopped. I just didn't trust the church. I have been away long enough that I am just starting to feel I can come back. (Absent Believer 22, Anglican)

One is aware that he is returning with a different, more adult understanding of faith:

I am starting to seek answers again at age 30, but I demand more from myself. God is no longer a "bell boy" that I call on when I'm trouble. I try to meet him a least halfway, before I even consider calling for help. (Absent Believer 30, United)

One father writes after his children have been at camp:

I hope to be going to church as a family soon. (Absent Believer 34, Baptist)

A SUPERNATURAL COMPONENT?

In answer to the question of what it might take to bring Absent Believers back to church, three people suggest that what is really needed is an initiative on the part of God:

What would it take? A miracle. (Absent Believer 34, Baptist)

Sometimes I think that I should re-embark on the spiritual journey. But do we ever leave? I guess I'm still waiting for God . . . I think God has to somehow intervene. Actually saying this seems like a cop-out. But I don't really know what else it would take. (Absent Believer 30, Presbyterian)

My own heart [would prompt a return], not to mention someone called GOD. (Absent Believer 23, Christian and Missionary Alliance)

Some of the stories told in the following chapter suggest that sometimes this kind of divine "nudge" actually happens.

AN UNSTABLE CATEGORY

My suspicion is that, for most Absent Believers, this will prove to be a transitional state, one that is difficult to maintain indefinitely. It is an unstable position to be in—spiritually, because Christianity is not a solitary religion but a social one ("You can't be a lone ranger Christian"); and sociologically, since our beliefs tend to be either reinforced or undermined by the community around us. It may be that for some, a "partial church substitute"—a small discussion group of like-minded Christians, for example, or a group who come together in social service—will enable them to maintain their faith more or less indefinitely. But the great majority of Absent Believers are not in that kind of support group.

Because of this, I find I make a distinction between "hard" and "soft" Absent Believers. The "hard" are those who will likely resolve the tensions that go with being an Absent Believer by giving up Christian faith altogether and becoming Former Believers. From the stories told by Former Believers, at least some went through a stage of being Absent Believers before they gave up Christianity altogether. "Soft" Absent Believers, on the other hand, are those who will find some way to resolve their quarrel with the church (or with God) and return to being Loyal Believers.

Some Absent Believers have already returned to church, on their own terms, and now identify themselves as Loyal Believers again. The next chapter will tell something of their stories.

8

TEMPORARY DETOUR

Why do Loyal Believers become
Absent Believers, then come back?

Daniel grew up in a United Church home, and Pioneer Camp was his first exposure to evangelical faith. He made a lot of friends there, and, when he went to university, took the opportunity to get involved with a campus fellowship and to attend the nearby Christian Missionary Alliance church that a lot of Christian students favoured. After graduation, however, he got a job in a city where he did not know many people. He tried attending a few churches, but found none that appealed to him or where there were people he could befriend. As a result, he began to drift from his Christian convictions, and got into a way of life he did not pretend was Christian. Three years later, his company transferred him to a new city, where he found himself in an office with a Christian he had known from university. The friend invited Daniel to go with him to an Anglican church, where Daniel found people his own age and with his own interests. The worship was lively, the preaching was thoughtful and mind-stretching, and Daniel decided it was time to get back into

Christian faith. He met the woman who is now his wife there, and together they have started a Bible study for couples of their age.

The survey asked Loyal Believers, "Have you had significant periods of time (six months or more) away from church and/or Christian faith?" One-third of them (83 out of 251) say they did.[1] What seems initially strange is that, in many ways, those Loyal Believers who took "time out" are quite similar to those who did not. The same sort of factors keep them in the faith, and they are active in their churches in comparable ways.

However, there are some generally small differences between Loyal Believers who have never been away and this second group I call Returned Believers. Those differences can be summarized by saying that Returned Believers:

- are somewhat less likely to have had spiritual mentors
- have been less helped by their study of the Bible—or perhaps have simply read it less
- are slightly more likely to have found help with the intellectual questions of Christian faith—like the Absent Believers they once were
- are somewhat less likely to value the fact that Christianity offers answers to life's big questions (questions of identity, meaning, purpose, and so on).
- have more often been helped by switching to a new church or denomination
- are less likely to have been influenced by the example of their parents
- are more likely to say that finding a life partner has been a very significant factor in maintaining their faith.

---

1. Other research has found the same: "46% of American Christians drop out of active religious participation for at least two years during some part of their lifetime . . . Most dropouts return to church involvement at a later time . . . Roozen estimated that about 80% would do so at some time (a very rough estimate)." Hoge in Bromley, 90.

The similarities and differences first show up when we look at what Returned Believers say maintains their faith. (See Figure 16.) As with Loyal Believers, relationships come top of the list, with God and with others.

It is interesting to compare not only the statistics, but also the comments, of Returned Believers with those of Loyal Believers:

My relationship with God

If "my relationship with God" is the number one factor that keeps people in the faith, it is not surprising to find that some say the lack

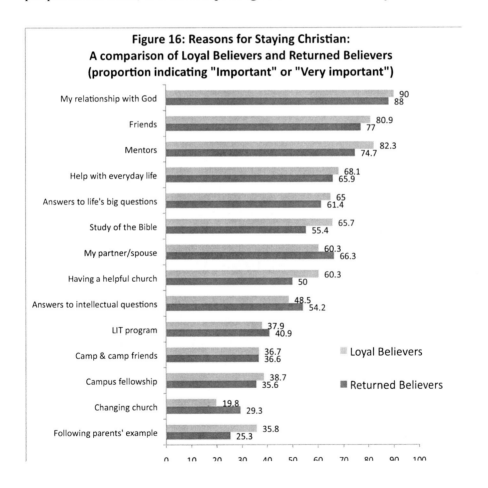

Figure 16: Reasons for Staying Christian:
A comparison of Loyal Believers and Returned Believers
(proportion indicating "Important" or "Very important")

of that relationship was what caused them to move away from faith. A few say things like this:

> Most of the times that I considered giving up . . . were when I doubted the relational aspects. This was almost always due to a long period of failing to seek intimacy with God—forgetting or having other subtle, higher priorities. (Returned Believer 24, Anglican to non-denominational)

However, the vast majority of Returned Believers say their relationship with God is what kept them in the faith through their "time away." As we saw with Loyal Believers, the unsolicited comments of Returned Believers about their relationship with God are vivid and authentic, and reflect great depth of conviction:

> I will truly never consider giving up my belief in JC. Every day is his and the focus of each day foremost is him. I couldn't "do" life without Christ at the helm. (Returned Believer 38, Presbyterian to Baptist)

> God is. Where else am I going to go? (Returned Believer 33, Anglican)

> I've discovered that God never will leave you or forsake you . . . If you try to run away from him he will follow, and he will never stop calling out to you. God is totally relentless. He's like the Terminator, only with facial expressions and without the Austrian accent. (Returned Believer 29, Baptist to Mennonite)

As with Loyal Believers, it seems as though for Returned Believers the sense of a real relationship with God covers a multitude of other difficulties. This is particularly interesting since almost one-third (31.3%) of Returned Believers also say that one of their major difficulties in faith has been a sense of unreality in their relationship with God. This is almost twice the number to be found among Loyal Believers (16.8%). Presumably these comments relate to different points in their lives. The data does not give detail on this, but my hunch is that the unreality of their relationship with

God was a factor in pushing them away for a time, and that when they speak of the importance of their relationship with God, they are speaking about the present.

The Christian community

As with Loyal Believers, the power of the Christian community to provide spiritual stability is very significant for Returned Believers. One puts it this way:

> The most important thing about the last years and maintaining a growing faith was relationship—having people to walk with on the journey—this includes people as well as God. (Returned Believer 30, Presbyterian to Baptist)

However, here is the first big difference. As we saw above, on every factor relating to community, Returned Believers consistently give lower ratings than Loyal Believers, though the differences are not always huge. Specifically, this group is less likely to have had Christian friends or mentors, a helpful church, a campus fellowship, or even to rate their family as helpful. I do not have enough data to say whether this absence of community was simply because their life circumstances changed, or whether they deliberately moved away from community, though it would be interesting to know. My guess is that there would be examples of each.

The only measure where Returned Believers give a higher rating to the influence of community is when they talk about a spouse/partner or children. Though it is not a large difference, they rate the importance of a spouse/partner at 66.3%, compared with 60.3% among Loyal Believers. It is more noticeable that, when they are asked how important having children has been to their staying in faith, 32.4% of Returned Believers say it was "important" or "very important," compared with only 21.2% among Loyal Believers.

What this suggests is that Returned Believers moved away from church and/or faith for a time at least in part because they had less community (whether intentionally or unintentionally). Then, when they got married and had children, they followed the well-worn trail back to church.

Friends

One sociologist, Kirk Hadaway, has observed that:

> If a child has close friends in the church with whom he or she can talk about spiritual matters, then the influence of peers will be a positive factor in the child's religious development.[2]

Of Returned Believers, 77.7% identify "friends" as "important" or "very important" in their faith.[3] Who are these friends? Returned Believers, somewhat more than Loyal Believers, say that they are "as close as ever" to friends they made at camp, that is, when they were teenagers. Maybe the fact that they were from outside the world of the teenager's home church was part of what made them helpful. The down side of this, however, is that faith was too closely associated with the world of camp, which some refer to as a "bubble," so that when they grew too old for camp, the bubble burst, and there was no other natural community that they were connected with.

Loyal Believers, on the other hand, for various reasons managed to make Christian friends not connected with the world of camp—perhaps in a campus fellowship or in their local church—and perhaps this was a factor helping them transfer into church involvement later. (See Figure 17.)

The other thing worth noting is that friends of Returned Believers often play a significant part in their "coming back." We will return to this later.

---

2. Hadaway 95.

3. This compares with 80.9% for Loyal Believers—not a significant difference.

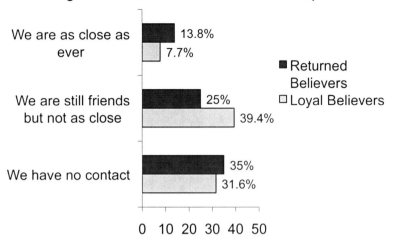

Figure 17: Who still has friends from camp?

First, however, let us look at what Returned Believers say about their experience of moving away.

WHAT CHALLENGED THE FAITH OF RETURNED BELIEVERS?

The complaints of this group are similar in many respects to the complaints of both Loyal Believers, but there are also significant differences. The two groups are similar in their responses to the following questions:

- neither group rates pressure from peers, or from a dating partner who believed differently, as a strong challenge to their faith
- both groups rated the high expectations of church involvement on the low end of the spectrum, around 10% or 11%.
- neither group felt strongly that they needed to pull away from faith in order to distinguish themselves from their parents: they rate this challenge at between 2% and 5%.
- there is only a small difference in how the two groups rate the significance of a personal "catastrophe" for faith: Returned Believers rate it at 12.5%, Loyal Believers at 8.6%. (Having said that, those

who do rate it highly have important things to say about their experience. I will discuss that later in the chapter.)

Where the differences between the two groups show up is illustrated by Figure 18:

Returned Believers were clearly more troubled by certain issues than Loyal Believers. Some of the differences are startlingly large. The biggest contrasts were these:

By a ratio of roughly three to one, Returned Believers were more likely than Loyal Believers to be challenged by:

a) moving away from Christian community (31.3% compared with 10.5%)

Figure 18: Challenges to Faith
Loyal Believers compared with Returned Believers
(proportion indicating "Important" or "Very important")

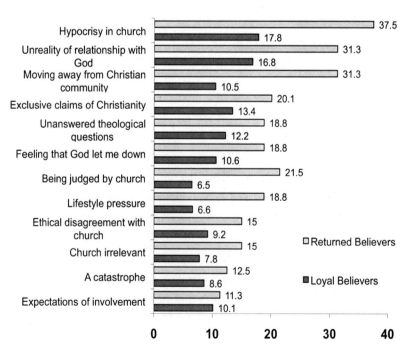

b) the feeling that they were being judged by the church (21.5% compared with 6.5%), and

c) lifestyle choices that were different from the expectations of their church (18.8% compared with 6.6%).

By a ratio of two to one, Returned Believers were more likely to be challenged by:

a) hypocrisy in the church (37.5% compared with 17.8%)

b) a sense of unreality in their relationship with God (31.3% compared with 16.8%), and

c) the feeling that church was irrelevant (15% compared with 7.8%).

These contrasts prepare us to hear what Returned Believers say about their move away from faith and/or church. As we would expect, there are strong correlations between the challenges to their faith and the reasons they left.

WHY DID THEY LEAVE?

Problems with church

The largest number of written comments (30) concerns problems with the church.[4] Many have felt let down, betrayed, or hurt by churches. Some may feel that some of these people gave up too easily on the church, and there may be cases in which that is a fair criticism. In fact, one person actually admits this:

> For several years I did not regularly attend Sunday church services, largely, I believe, because I developed contempt for

---

4. Gibbs and Brierley found that in the UK and Australia around 50% left because of problems with the church, including boredom, loneliness and irrelevance. Gibbs, 289. Hoge found that one-third of people who left did so because of "disagreement with religious doctrine, perceptions of hypocrisy among church members, or loss of faith." Hoge 47.

the church as representatives/institutions of the Christian Faith. I think this was due to a very conceited view of being able to maintain faith without a stable faith community supporting the individual—a "My faith is strong enough and mature enough that I don't need a church" type of view. (Returned Believer 28, Anglican to Vineyard)

This is very honest, and shows a high level of self-awareness. Probably others could say the same. Nevertheless, as before, the remaining comments are so many in number and often so stark that it seems fair to say that the fault was not usually on the side of the respondent. I have divided the comments into broad categories:

Lack of appropriate caring[5]

Husband's burnout/illness » physical, spiritual, emotional » directly related to the church, betrayal by church community. (Returned Believer 38, Christian Reformed)

I didn't receive any support from the church when I was struggling at home with an alcoholic father, because he was also a member of the church. (Returned Believer 29, Baptist to United)

This year has been a rough one—moving to a new city and starting to be involved in a church, but having people openly shun you there. That has been a first for me. (Returned Believer 22, Anglican to Christian and Missionary Alliance)

Hypocrisy

I feel like the church I grew up in measured your faith and salvation (even though they preached it was by grace) by what you did. (Returned Believer 29, Baptist to Presbyterian)

---

5. In the UK, 20% of church-leavers "disengage from church feeling that they have been let down by the church" (Francis and Richter, 218). Jamieson also identifies people who have experienced disappointment and hurt at not receiving care which was promised or implied by the church. They belong to a group he calls "Disillusioned Followers" (Jamieson, 50).

Seeing the church, its hypocrisies and unkindnesses towards non-Christians, through the eyes of my non-Christian (then) boyfriend. (Returned Believer 25, Baptist to Anglican)

Lack of relevance:

I have spent time away from church because the church my family goes to really does not speak to me. It is very small and mostly older people (50+) and all the songs we sing are old hymns. A lot of the teachings are geared toward the older crowd, and I find that I cannot relate a lot. (Returned Believer 22, non-denominational)

Feeling dissatisfied with the church, tired of hearing the same explanations to complex questions, dissatisfied with Christian culture and jargon. (Returned Believer 30, Baptist to Anglican)

It is interesting that, where church problems are concerned, Absent Believers have very similar issues to these Returned Believers: hypocrisy, misuse of power, failure to love, petty legalism, and so on. The difference is that the Returned Believers have somehow made their way back to church life. We will look at the question of how and why they have done so later.

Time at university

Fifteen of those eighty-three Returned Believers (18%) write in comments about the significance of university in their moving away from active faith. This in line with Reg Bibby's observation that "Considerable numbers of people who were raised in the church drop out during their late teens and early 20s."[6] What Hoge says about mainline young people at university also applies to those from conservative Christian homes:

---

6. Bibby 1995, 75. Cf. Brierley says of the UK and Australia: "[I]t is frightening to think that half of those who leave the church do so before the age of 20" (Gibbs, 286).

Today mainline Protestant young people attend college in great numbers, and in the process they acquire worldviews and values inconsistent with their hometown church experiences.[7]

The challenges of university for Christians included:

- stress
- pressure on time
- the enjoyment of independence
- difficulty in finding a suitable church
- not liking the student fellowships
- the challenge of new worldviews and
- laziness.[8]

To put these things in their own words, Returned Believers say that they left church/faith because of:

The stress of higher learning and the limited time available to keep connected with a church (Returned Believer 34, Anglican)

A move away to College, a new city, an opportunity to reinvent myself. (Returned Believer 34, Anglican)

During my first year of university, I just simply found myself gradually becoming more and more lazy in all aspects of my life including my faith. (Returned Believer 28, Catholic)

I went to university and had trouble finding a church that was easy to get to that I liked—and I was hung over!! (Returned Believer 25, Baptist)

---

7. Hoge, 164

8. Hoge found that "The principal reasons our respondents gave for dropping out had to do with matters of personal convenience and lifestyle changes. Thirty-two percent told us they became inactive because they had left home and family; another 31 percent dropped out because of time constraints or 'laziness'." Ibid., 47.

Some are more specific about lifestyle pressures. Three in particular link these directly with moving away from Christian community:

> After first year university . . . I felt that Christianity, and more specifically the Christians I knew, were causing me to miss out on the "university experience". I felt that the Christians I knew expected me not to drink, only talk to Christians, dress a certain way etc. (Returned Believer 32, Anglican to Associated Gospel Church)

> From age 17-21 I got deeper and deeper into sin primarily from lack of a strong influential church and Christian peer group to influence me, dating non-believers . . . drinking, smoking, drugs, sex . . . I wanted to experiment with what the world had to offer. (Returned Believer 30, Anglican to Christian and Missionary Alliance)

> "Good times" at university, and a lack of accountability to Christian friends, church, etc. (Returned Believer 27, Baptist to Presbyterian)

Some did not find student fellowships helpful:

> Those groups seemed to contain the "castoffs" from all the other social groups. If every other clique wouldn't accept you, then those Christians would. (Returned Believer 30, Christian Missionary Alliance)

One might argue that it is one role of Christians to be a community for the "castoffs" of the world. However, at least one Returned Believer was disappointed with the campus fellowship for more substantial reasons. She simply wanted the help of other Christians to figure out questions of life and faith which were bothering her at this point in her life, but did not find it:

> During university I became aware of issues I hadn't really thought about, cultures I had not seen, people I had not met etc. I began to doubt and ponder what Christianity meant to me and,

unfortunately, was met with indifference and, at times, scorn from the Christian community (IVCF, Church, camp). This only served to drive me further away. It was an intense period of questioning and reflecting on God, the church and my role as a Christian in the world. (Returned Believer 36, Baptist)

This person's story is very different from the previous examples. Here is someone not wanting to experiment with "the world," but asking important questions about life and faith, and not finding help. This is particularly disappointing when it involves a campus fellowship of other students, who might be expected to be dealing with the same questions.

Several times so far, respondents have made a distinction between church and faith. Once again in these comments, several emphasize that what they were leaving was only church, not faith itself:

What I have frequently felt like "giving up on" has been church—not Christian faith. (Returned Believer 33, Baptist to Anglican)

[During] my four years in university, I did not always go to church, but I wouldn't say I was not a Christian at this point— struggling somewhat, but not away. (Returned Believer 32, Christian Reformed)

Most of my difficulty with Christianity has been with the church. I am sometimes so frustrated by community. I have never considered taking a break from God. My relationship with him isn't dependent on church. (Returned Believer 30, Presbyterian to Baptist)

During this time my relationship with God was unaffected. (Returned Believer 27, Baptist to Mennonite)

I didn't leave the faith, I merely stopped attending church. (Returned Believer 26, Methodist to Baptist)

During that time period, however, I don't feel that I ever really moved away from the Christian faith. I just felt that there wasn't a great need for me to go to church. (Returned Believer 25, Baptist to Christian and Missionary Alliance)

It was truly my faith that kept me going when I did not have the people present to help. (Returned Believer 25, none to non-denominational)

Moving

Like Absent Believers, Returned Believers illustrate the truth of Reginald Bibby's statement that moving is a disruptive influence on people's involvement in church.[9] Of Returned Believers, almost one-third (31.3%) say their leaving church was connected with moving (only 10.5% of Loyal Believers said this was a problem). Fourteen take the trouble to write comments about this. They say this kind of thing:

Moving around a lot has made it difficult at times to feel closely affiliated with a church. (Loyal Believer 30, United)

Living in a new city, without transportation, and trying to find a new body of believers to go to church with frustrated me. (Returned Believer 22, Anglican to Christian and Missionary Alliance)

Whether we like it or not, not all churches are created equal, and a person moving from a church they like in one city may not find a similar one, even of the same denomination, in the next. It is not that the churches are not there: it is rather that they are not a good fit in some way:

I still struggle with finding a church that helps me worship God. If only I could escape the song, "Shine, Jesus, Shine"!!! (Returned Believer 30, Baptist to Anglican)

---

9. Bibby 1995, 78. Cf. In Gibbs and Brierley's research, 46% of leavers said they "moved out of the area and did not look for a new church." Gibbs 289.

Moving to a small town, where churches seem to lack an active worship focus was hard. (Returned Believer 26, Baptist)

Last year I moved to another city to attend school, and finding a church has been a bit of a problem. I have now found one, but it is very different from what I have become accustomed to and isn't totally helpful to my faith because it caters to VERY new Christians and isn't much of a challenge. (Returned Believer 25, Baptist to non-denominational)

At this point, many people solve the problem by changing denomination (remember that that two-thirds of respondents have changed denomination since they were teenagers). Thus one Baptist says he:

Moved to a new town, and was unable to find a church that I wanted to attend. (Returned Believer 32, Baptist to Presbyterian)

He says later that it was when he moved to yet another city that he found a church he felt he could get involved in—presumably the Presbyterian one he now associates with.

Even when people are eager to get involved in a new church, it takes time:

I have just moved to [a new city] and spent the fall finding a church. My husband, daughter and I just decided in January on a church, so we have not yet gotten involved. (Returned Believer 32, Anglican to Mennonite)

For those who complain of "lack of community" and particularly the fourteen who describe the problems of moving, this is often what they are referring to when they say they spent "six months or more" away from church. For them, it was not necessarily a failure of the church, not anything doctrinal, not an ethical dilemma, and not an experience of suffering. It was simply the difficulty of finding the right church in a new town. As Bibby points out, this is a major problem for churches. In the next chapter, I will suggest one way churches could respond.

Suffering

When they were asked what had challenged their faith, one-eighth (12.5%) of Returned Believers said that suffering was an "Important" or "Very Important" factor. Six describe how suffering pushed them away from church and/or faith. They say things like:

> I was dealing with my Mom's death. She had been a very committed Christian and had helped me anchor my Christian walk. When she was gone I felt like my anchor slipped and as a result of this I drifted for about 2-3 years. (Returned Believer 38, Anglican to Baptist)

> [I left because of] Personal grief over a relationship loss. (Returned Believer 30, Anglican to Associated Gospel Church)

> Several people died that I knew: two of my friends' moms . . . my great aunt and uncle who I was very close to; and my roommate's fiancée committed suicide. These all took place with a six month period that year and I really struggled with seeing any hope in all the sadness. (Returned Believer 27, Baptist to Presbyterian)

> The process of grieving the death of my former partner eventually involved my leaving the church where we met. (Returned Believer 26, United)

One struggled with whether to give up, but managed to hang in:

> I don't think I ever abandoned God and the Christian church. I did have a period of depression over 6 months (a serious breakup, insecurity about the future, dissatisfaction with the church), but I still held on to God and went grudgingly to church (and kept helping with youth group) if only to wait on God for the next step in my life. (Returned Believer 26, Lutheran to Christian and Missionary Alliance)

Others of course have experiences of suffering, but not everybody moves away from faith because of it. There seems to be no pattern as to why some people leave because of suffering and others do not. Certainly there are some who leave because of anger and feeling let down by God. Others simply seem to deal with problems better alone. What is interesting is how few leave church and faith for ever because of such experiences.

WHAT RETURNED BELIEVERS DO NOT SAY

Conventional wisdom says that young people from religious homes cannot wait to get away in order to experiment with new thoughts and new behaviors. One Returned Believer actually verbalizes this:

> Many people who are raised in a Christian environment/home go through a period of rebellion in which they must test for themselves if the values they have been living by are truly their own. (Returned Believer 29, Baptist to Free Methodist)

But even in her case, this is simply a theory. The desire for independence was not a factor in her own moving away. In fact, only 2.6% of Returned Believers say "the need to be different from my parents" was an "Important" or "Very important" factor in driving them from church and/or faith.[10] The other factors we have looked at—disillusionment with church, the attractions of university life, and moving—all count as far more significant challenges.

---

10. This compares with 5.2% of Loyal Believers who say the need to be different from their parents challenged their faith, and only 1.9% of Absent Believers, who say the need to be different from their parents was one factor in moving them away from church/faith.

WHAT CAUSES PEOPLE TO RETURN?[11]

The reasons Returned Believers come back are many and complex. (See Figure 19.) Not surprisingly, most talk about more than one factor. The most common are:

- a spiritual crisis
- finding a new Christian community
- marriage and children, and
- the influence of friends and family.

Of these four, the three human factors (community, marriage and friends) have been well documented by sociologists. What they do not usually look at is the spiritual dimension, but, at least in this

Figure 19: What brought Returned Believers back? (Numbers commenting on each factor)

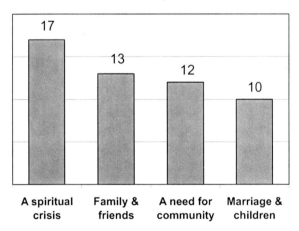

11. I was not expecting such a high rate of response to the question, "Have you had significant periods of time (six months or more) away from church and/ or Christian faith?" and so did not offer a range of standard responses for people to check. As a result, I am dependent in what follows on respondents' write-in comments. Fortunately, they are plentiful and detailed. It is probably worth underscoring the fact that the vast majority answered about time away from church rather than time way from faith.

research, it is the most common reason for people to return. The stories people tell along these lines are surprising and intriguing.

A spiritual awakening

The largest number of written responses (seventeen) describe a spiritual crisis or awakening as the thing which prompted them to return. Some involve a spiritual awakening and a considered decision that it was simply time to return:

> We recognized that God was doing a huge thing in our lives—
> that ultimately it's not about committees, DOING things, or
> the church. It's about walking with God and BEING a child of
> God. We found a community where this was valued. (Returned
> Believer 38, Christian Reformed)

> My life was no better without God than with him. In fact I was
> making a mess of it myself (in an unhealthy relationship with a
> non-Christian man). I decided to try going back after I broke up
> with this man . . . I am so glad I went back. (Returned Believer
> 32, Anglican to Associated Gospel Church)

> I had felt that there wasn't a great need for me to go to church.
> Then I made a decision to start going to church again. I just felt
> it was time to start going again. I suppose it was God telling me
> that by not going to church I was in effect starving myself spiri-
> tually. (Returned Believer 25, Baptist)

Others describe a general feeling of dissatisfaction with things:

> My life felt less joyful, purposeful, meaningful. (Returned
> Believer 24, Anglican to non-denominational)

There is a significant group, however, for whom the return is quite dramatic:

> I was held up at gunpoint at work one night. In order to deal
> with the post traumatic stress disorder I turned to the minister
> of the church I grew up in. (Returned Believer 34, Anglican)

A friend's death pushed me into a discussion with God. In a 4-5 hour drive home from the funeral—I was yelling at him—and I heard him talk back (to my surprise). He provided some direction and I re-started my search. (Returned Believer 34, Baptist to Anglican)

I hit rock bottom—all that I thought was important was destroyed—my integrity, my skills, my relationships, even my faith, yet it was then that I experienced the presence of God like never before. (Returned Believer 31, Baptist to Congregational)

God won me back through: convicting me of my sin through Scripture and the work of the Holy Spirit as a result of the prayers of my family and one or two Christian friends; the love of a few consistent and passionate followers of Christ that I met at university. (Returned Believer 30, Anglican to Christian and Missionary Alliance)

At the end of that year away I had a great moment of spiritual cleansing and clarity. At one point all of my sins just came crashing down on me in a wave of emotion. (Returned Believer 28, Catholic)

Saw the person I was becoming and hated it. Finally realized that I was a sinner and that I needed a savior. God removed me from my environment for 10 weeks. It allowed me to reflect upon my life and where it was going. It was a time where God continually revealed himself to me. (Returned Believer 23, Christian and Missionary Alliance to Presbyterian)

A vivid experience of the presence of the Holy Spirit. (Returned Believer 27, Baptist)

God pulled me back. (Returned Believer 27, Baptist to Presbyterian)

During my first year of university, I felt called, in a very personal and profound way, back to a relationship with God. (Returned Believer XX, Anglican to Congregational)

A person who had five people close to him die within the space of six months wrote of:

Experiencing a real need for God and perhaps for the first time a true sense of his presence in my despair. (Returned Believer 27, Baptist to Presbyterian)

He speaks now of a stronger faith: "I feel that, having gone through a serious time of doubt and questioning, I now have a stronger faith. Before this turning, it was easier to fake my faith."

The range of these experiences is broad and unpredictable: a life falling apart, being held up at gunpoint, the death of friends and family, the love of friends, a sense of self-loathing. All of them are classic spiritual situations to which Christianity offers help, yet each one sounds quite unique and not one sounds clichéd.

The Absent Believer who commented about his own potential return, "I think God has to somehow intervene" may be uncomfortably close to the truth. As one respondent commented:

God reveals himself to those who have given up, that's part of the story. (Returned Believer 26, Baptist to non-denominational)

Of course, this is frustrating for people in ministry, who would like to organize programs to help young people return to church and faith. If so much is dependent on God's initiative, there is not much that can be organized! But this is the reality, which Christianity has always affirmed: God is at work to draw people into relationship. We can resist and even refuse, or we can co-operate and even assist. The fact remains that it is not solely our job to bring it about.

While this is hard for the activist pastor or youth worker (or even a concerned parent), it also brings a healthy perspective. Among other things, it reminds us that human beings are not "market units," to be lured into a response that they do not really choose. Neither is the conversion of young people (or anybody else for that matter) primarily a human responsibility. In fact, there is a peacefulness that comes from acknowledging God's initiative in these matters.

This does not mean there is nothing for church workers to do, of course: the church still has to work at being what churches are called to be, and the new wine of renewed faith needs the new wine skins of Christian community. In fact, many Returned Believers speak about just such a need:

A need for community

A significant number (twelve), during their time away, simply came to realize the importance of church for the Christian life:

> I kept messing up and realized that Christ, whom I still loved, had been pretty clear about His body as part of the solution. (Returned Believer 38, Baptist to non-denominational)

> The book The Body by Chuck Colson[12] painted a 'glorious picture' of something worth striving for and believing in. Christian friends and family were very nonjudgmental also. (Returned Believer 30, Anglican to Associated Gospel Church)

> I . . . realized that community is an important part of living as God has asked us to live. I am drawn to community at the same time as I want to run from it. Somehow God is present in the midst of His flawed and sometimes crazy body of believers. So, I choose to continue to be in community, although at times kicking and screaming. (Returned Believer 30, Presbyterian to Baptist)

> I realized that church is about God, not me. I found a new church. (Returned Believer 29, Baptist to Mennonite)

> I found a church that fed me and became an incredible family to me. (Returned Believer 26, Methodist to Baptist)

> I grew up and realized that it was important to me to attend church and to be a part of a Christian community. (Returned Believer 24, Presbyterian)

---

12. Charles Colson and Ellen Santilli Vaughn, *The Body* (Dallas TX: Word Publishing, 1994).

My relationship with God . . . suffered desperately through
a lack of significant community and close Christian friends.
(Returned Believer 24, Baptist to Anglican)

I had several years without attending church regularly—I did
not think I needed to go to church to have a relationship with
God . . . I believe the Lord called me back to a closer relationship with him through friends and other influences. I began to
desire to go deeper with him and meet with a group of believers
regularly. (Returned Believer 24, Baptist)

Guilt pressure from Mom, a need for community. (Returned
Believer XX, XX)

For most of these, although the experience is not as dramatic as
the stories of the previous group, it is clear that their relationship
with God is a factor in motivating the return. It is not simply a case
of people saying, "I wanted my children to learn about God"; it is
more along the lines of their saying, "I felt God was telling me . . ."
If they had not had this sense of a relationship with God through the
"time away," the return might not have been so clear cut, or indeed
might not have happened at all.

On a more mundane level, returning to church is often as simple
as finding a new, more congenial church. We have noted already how
mobility cuts down on people's commitment to church. But some of
these Returned Believers show that mobility also has a positive side.
Moving can be an opportunity to lose touch with one church, but it
can just as easily be an occasion for finding a new one. Not that this
makes it easy. More than one, realising that finding the right church
is a serious business, took time to do research before making a commitment. But moving does open up some fresh options.

Took a long time deciding what I type of church I wanted to
attend and spent time talking to others who really enjoyed their
church. Returned to attending after 6 months and spent more
time exploring many churches before staying at one in particular. (Returned Believer 37, Anglican to Christian and Missionary Alliance)

We wanted a church within a community that we could raise our children and be witnesses in. God moved us . . . and showed us a new church where we are contributing more than we have ever before. (Returned Believer 33, Christian Reformed to Associated Gospel Church)

Coming back to the area where my family lived and reconnecting with a church and making a stronger commitment to live out my faith. (Returned Believer 31, Baptist)

We still had a deep desire to be part of a church since we still had deep Christian faith individually and jointly and searched until we found a church that isn't ghettoized and encourages us to grow in our faith. (Returned Believer 28, United to Quaker)

It's been slow. Changing cities and finding a new community, with a few close Christian friends, has helped immensely. (Returned Believer 25, Baptist to Anglican)

Many Returned Believers—thirteen in all—say that friends and family are one of the factors that helped them move back into a Christian community. Others say friends and family are the most important factor. Judging by the comments about camp friends above, at least some of the friends who helped the transition to a new church will have been from the world of camp. When asked what brought Returned Believers back, they say:

Friends and family, including partner . . . encouraged me to get back involved/in touch. (Returned Believer 34, Anglican)

Reconnecting with old friends and meeting new friends who share my faith. (Returned Believer 36, Baptist to Presbyterian)

I found good Christian friends who went to a wonderful church. I started to go and quickly entered back into my faith. (Returned Believer 30, Baptist to Pentecostal)

A friend in university who invited me to her church, which was much more contemporary than the one I was technically a member of but didn't attend. I enjoyed the music, and there were people my age. (Returned Believer 29, Presbyterian)

My friend knew what God wanted of her and was able to help me out and be a support for me. A lot of what she said was hurtful—she has never been particularly tactful—but it was grounded in truth. (Returned Believer 26, Methodist to Baptist)

A friend with a car took me to a good church and then I got my own car. (Returned Believer 25, Baptist)

Changing cities and finding a new community, with a few close Christian friends, has helped immensely. (Returned Believer 24, Baptist to Anglican)

Marriage and children

Ten speak of wanting to return to church because of marriage and children:

Getting married, finding a church that was Christ-centered and then having children and wanting them to first know the Lord in an everyday way has all contributed to my commitment to our church. (Returned Believer 38, Presbyterian to Baptist)

Got married, went to Bible College. (Returned Believer 36, Christian and Missionary Alliance)

I find that my wife and I have renewed interest in the growth of our faith since the birth of our first child. We definitely drifted away from regular church attendance in the first few years of our marriage. I gave up the job that had me traveling five days a week; and when our son was born we wanted to make sure that he grew up in a practicing Christian home. (Returned Believer 32, Catholic)

Other people who have researched the faith journey of young people have observed how important marriage and family are for coming back to church.[13] What is interesting about these respon-

---

13. E.g. Hoge, Johnson and Luidens, 40.

dents, however, is that other factors, not least the "spiritual" ones, rank far more highly on the list of reasons for coming back.

A painful return

Although many of these stories sound and often are joyful, returning may sometimes be difficult, just as the leaving was painful. These are comments from someone deeply hurt by her previous church:

> My return to the church has been a gradual and tentative process. I have had to take baby steps and test for levels of trust along the way. Today I attend church and just this September I became involved in a small group. This is very scary for me but I know that God is telling me to re-engage and forgive. (Loyal Believer 27, Baptist to Mennonite)

Those longing to welcome returning believers back need to be clear about the welcome, of course. Yet at the same time they need to be aware that it takes courage to come back to a place associated with previous bad experiences. Enthusiasm will need to be tempered by sensitivity.

HOW FAR ARE RETURNED BELIEVERS INVOLVED IN THEIR CHURCHES?

Some research suggests that once people have had "time away" from church and return, they will be less involved than they were during their first involvement. For example, Peter Brierley found that in the UK and Australia:

> Those who have left and subsequently returned tend to go to church slightly less now than those who have never left . . . In other words, once the commitment is broken it is difficult to recover it.[14]

---

14. Gibbs, 286.

I did not ask how often respondents go to church. But I did ask what aspects of church life they are now involved in, which seems a more important measurement. When we compare the involvement of Returned Believers with that of Loyal Believers, there are some differences, but it is not that Loyal Believers are more involved.

Figure 20: What church activities do Loyal Believers and Returned Believers engage in?

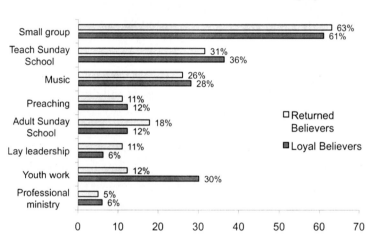

(See Figure 19.) The gap is not huge, but Returned Believers are somewhat more likely (6% more) to be involved in lay leadership positions and adult Sunday School. Loyal Believers, on the other hand, are slightly more likely (5% more) to teach Sunday School.

The one place where there is a noticeable difference is involvement in youth ministry (30.1% compared with 12.3%), which is heavily dominated by Loyal Believers. The most likely explanation is that Returned Believers were absent during the time that young adults are generally asked to help with youth group leadership.

Apart from that, however, there is no noticeable difference between the level of involvement of Returned Believers and that of Loyal Believers. This is not what Brierley found, so why might there be this difference among this group? My hunch is that the majority of these respondents were brought up (at home and certainly at camp) with models and teaching that the Christian life by its nature involves "servant leadership," which is often demanding. Thus, when they decide to return to church, they do so with an understanding that this will mean commitment to the church's ministries.

SO WHAT?

This leads into the question of what the church can learn from all this. How can churches respond to the needs of younger people, living in the contemporary world, in a way that is authentically Christian and yet culturally sensitive? The question merits a chapter of its own.

9

TRAVELING TOGETHER

What Makes a Good Church?

Emily is dissatisfied with her church. In her own words:

> For the past two years I have been involved in the youth group
> at my parents' church as the only young adult who still attends
> church regularly and cares for the spiritual life of today's youth.
> I have slowly removed myself from other aspects of my parent's
> church since I was so frustrated with it. Now, if I could find a
> healthy Christian community, I would love to be involved in
> an adult Sunday school (it doesn't really exist in my parent's
> church), in music (at my parent's church the piano and organ
> are preferable to guitar), and I would certainly be involved in
> outreach activities. In short, if I could find a good church, I
> would be one of their most active members.[1]

*If I could find a good church, I would be one of their most active
members.* Here is a 26-year old who identifies herself as a Loyal
Believer. She has stuck it out in a difficult situation for a long time,

---

1. This is an actual quotation from one of the responses, but the name Emily
is fictional.

and is longing for fresh opportunities. I am not sure I would have the heart to tell her she needs to stay where she is indefinitely.

But when she finds "a good church," she is going to be a great asset to it. What pastor would not be delighted to have someone like Emily as part of their congregation? And, on a more gloomy note, what will happen to Emily if she does not find "a good church"?

Of course, the question is, What does Emily think is a good church? What are others of her generation looking for?[2] To probe this area, I asked a couple of questions. All the surveys asked the question: "What advice would you like to give to church leaders about the way they respond to young people?" Fifty-one respondents (most of them Loyal Believers) wrote answers to this question.

On the questionnaire for Absent Believers, I also asked, "What would be three characteristics of a church you can imagine wanting to join, if any?" Not surprisingly, every one of the fifty-six Absent Believers had something to say in answer to this question.

This chapter blends the answers to those questions, and I will add to the mix some reflections based on what the Loyal Believers said in earlier chapters about what has kept them in church.

The overwhelming impression from reading answers to these questions is that these people are not asking for the moon. Indeed, they are fairly tolerant people. They are not setting the bar particularly high. They have been around churches enough to know that churches are not perfect, and cannot be expected to be. They have probably laughed at the old saying, "If you find the perfect church, don't join it, because then it won't be perfect any more." They are not whiners, simply asking for everything to be just the way they like it. And neither are they asking churches to become something which churches were never meant to be.

---

2. Posterski and Barker's book, *Where's a Good Church?* is very helpful in addressing this issue in more detail.

Basically, what they are asking is that churches should try to behave like churches—which does not seem a lot to ask. Unfortunately, that has not been the experience of many. As you read these responses, ask yourself whether you agree with their picture of what churches should be like. And of course, it is worth asking the related question: why is it so difficult for churches to behave like churches?[3] When we ask, What can churches learn? this is perhaps the most important question.

There are four areas of church life in particular that respondents write about:

* community
* openness to questions and new ideas
* social activism, and
* the content and style of worship services.[4]

COMMUNITY

About ten actually use the term "community" to describe what they want in a church. Many others, however, seem to be describing the same thing in other terms. What they are looking for in a church is:

---

3. The assumed definition of church here is something like "the visible expression of the gathered followers of Jesus Christ who have been grafted into a community created by God, under the banner of Jesus Christ, embodying in an anticipatory way the life and values of the new creation." Allan J. McNicol, "Church", in *The Eerdmans Dictionary of the Bible*, ed. David Noel Freedman (Grand Rapids: Eerdmans, 2000), 254. The comments are not usually about denominations or about the worldwide church, but about individual, local churches.

4. There are some similarities between this list and that compiled by Posterski and Barker (19-48). They found that people wanted community, relevance, outreach and orthodoxy. The last of these four is not an emphasis among my respondents, though their comments about preaching are somewhat parallel.

Acceptance, fulfilling, a home and family away from home. (Absent Believer 28, Anglican to Christian and Missionary Alliance)

A sense of family; offers support and help for those who need it. (Absent Believer 28, Baptist)

A sense of belonging. (Absent Believer 24, United)

"Community," however, is a slippery word with a range of meanings. In Christian faith, the basic idea behind the term "community" is that the Christian life is meant to be a life lived with others. What God wants of the church is not a lot of isolated followers of Jesus, who just happen to get together at the same religious gas station to refill their spiritual gas tank on a Sunday morning. Rather, God is trying to bring into being a new kind of community to reflect God's own nature, which is Trinity. People generally join the community one by one, of course, but that is only the beginning. As David Watson used to put it, "If the Christian life does not begin with the individual, it does not begin. But if it ends with the individual, it ends."

The New Testament uses a number of pictures to make this point: it says the church is meant to be like a body—the Body of Christ— in which every member plays a unique part; it is like a family or household, of which God is the head; it is like a temple in which all the members are interdependent, like the stones in a wall; and so on. All these are trying to give ideas of unity, common purpose, mutual support, closeness, intimacy, and loyalty. And what marks this community off from any other is the fact that this community is trying to follow Jesus Christ.

Inclusiveness

When people go into details about what exactly they want in a Christian community, two emphases emerge. One is inclusiveness. Respondents look for a church that is:

Inclusive of all races, languages, classes and lifestyle choices. (Absent Believer 28, Catholic)

[Characterized by] A dedication to ALL believers and where they are at. (Absent Believer 24, Associated Gospel Church)

Allowing people to feel a sense of community and inclusion despite their lifestyles, that simply brings people together on the basis of their recognition of God and the truth of Christ's teachings. Accepting of people no matter what they are like. (Absent Believer 23, Catholic)

Certainly these concerns resonate with the New Testament's emphasis that in the church "there is no longer Jew or Greek, there is no longer slave or free, there is no longer male or female, for all of us are one in Jesus Christ."[5] Part of the point of what God is doing in the church is that it brings together people who would not otherwise give one another the time of day. Over time, God then forms them into a "body," serving God's purposes in the world.

Having said that, of course, there is (and perhaps always will be) a tension between inclusiveness and discipleship. Jesus' dinner parties were scandalous for their inclusiveness. Absolutely anybody was invited to sit at table with Jesus. But what is sometimes overlooked is that, of those people who sat with him and heard his message, not all went on to become disciples, because he made clear that following him meant a commitment to learn and to live in his way. Paul's words in Galatians do not include differences of "lifestyle." The challenge is to be discerning about which differences of lifestyle are compatible with being a follower of Jesus—and how far and how long to be patient with those differences which seem incompatible with discipleship.

But for most respondents who comment on this issue, the line is often drawn too far on the side of exclusion: things are made conditions of discipleship which are really only legitimate differences of lifestyle. I could not help noticing that these comments are from

---

5. Galatians 3:28 (NRSV)

members of more conservative denominations: Baptist, Christian and Missionary Alliance, Associated Gospel and Roman Catholic.

Authentic friendships

The other emphasis that appears time and again is related—the need for a community where one can be honest and vulnerable and not pretend. Words like "true" and "real" crop up. People want a church where:

> Real relationships are fostered, not forced and assigned and organized, but where people commit to love and support each other—a sharing of lives. (Absent Believer 22, Catholic)

> People share their true emotions and struggles instead of pretending that everything is OK. (Absent Believer 24, Baptist)

> I can be a someone but not always have to be "on my game." (Absent Believer 26, Congregational)

> "Real" Christians talking about doubt, failure and not finding God. (Absent Believer 23, non-denominational)

How can a church grow as this kind of community? One way is simply by encouraging friendship. Chapter 3 discussed the fact that 80.9% of Loyal Believers say that friends are "Important" or "Very important" for the fact that they have persevered in faith. Don Posterski cites a study which discovered something similar, that:

> the number of friendships developed in the first six months [in a church] is critical in maintaining and strengthening a relationship between the visitor and the new congregation. Of the active members surveyed in [the] study, all could name three or more friends made in the first six months . . . But of the 50 people who had left the church, eight had established no such relationships, 14 could name only one friend, and eight could name three friends.[6]

---

6. Posterski and Barker 33.

Most churches rate themselves as "friendly," but often the friendliness exists only between those who are already members, not towards newcomers. Many churches train their greeters to welcome new people, to help them find their way around, to speak to them after the service, and to inform them of the activities of the church. This is good. But there is a difference between the work of the official greeter and the sensitivity of an ordinary member who thinks, "Oh there's a new person. I'll go and talk to them." Friendly greeters are an important first step: a congregation that is prepared to offer genuine friendship to newcomers is even more important.[7]

How then does friendship grow? There is something mysterious and unpredictable about friendship: there are no ten quick rules for making and keeping a friend. But in general it requires knowing a person in more than one context. A relationship that begins at work over a shared task probably moves in the direction of friendship when people begin to meet outside the work place—over lunch or at the gym or going to a movie. Two people may enjoy working together on a church committee, but it is hardly feels like true friendship until it moves on to praying together or visiting one another's homes or having coffee or meeting at a party. There is a multi-dimensionality to true friendship, and that can only happen over time. Maybe we find so few friendships because, in a world of instant gratification, we do not find the time to let this kind of long-term relationship percolate.

Can churches be places where this kind of trusting, open friendship develops? Certainly friendship should be important for Christians because, as Paul Stevens points out:

---

7. I have written more about this topic in a booklet called *From Visitor to Disciple: Eight Ways Your Church Can Help* (Richmond, BC: Digory Publishing, 2005).

there is something like friendship in the Godhead since God is more "one" because of being three and not one in spite of being three. [8]

Indeed, one ancient writer paraphrased "God is love" as "God is friendship."[9] If Christians thought of friendship as being an essential part of their faith, and worked at growing friendships as a spiritual discipline, more people would be inclined to come to—and to stay in—our communities.

Mentors

You will remember that mentors were another reason people stayed within Christian faith. In fact, Loyal Believers identify mentors as slightly more important to their faith than friends— although mentoring is really a specialized form of friendship.[10] It would help people stick with their churches if the leaders made mentoring a normal part of the church's way of doing things, even for a mentoring program to be built into a church's regular program.

Yet, as one Loyal Believer wrote, "Mentors are extremely rare in the church, and the ones doing the mentoring are stretched very thin." This may in part be because the word "mentor" is itself intimidating. However, one does not need to be a spiritual giant or have a string of theology degrees in order to be a mentor. You simply need to be little older in the faith (and normally in years) than the other person. The first time I was asked to be a spiritual mentor, I was twenty, and had been a serious follower of Jesus for about four years. Tim was eighteen, and had been a follower

---

8. R. Paul Stevens, "Friendship" in *The Complete Book of Everyday Christianity* ed. Robert Banks and R. Paul Stevens (Downers Grove: InterVarsity Press, 1997), 436.

9. 1 John 4:16. Aelred of Rievaulx in the 13th century. Ibid. 437

10. Aelred classified mentoring as a "receptive friendship." Ibid., 437.

of Jesus for two years. Once a week we met to eat together, talk about life and God, puzzle over the Bible together and pray for one another. It was great, for me as much as for him.

Some respondents have already found a role as spiritual mentors:

> I meet one-on-one with a younger leader for prayer twice monthly. I also meet one-on-one with a young woman for Bible study and support to her ongoing counselling. (Loyal Believer 36, Anglican to Mennonite)

> I mentor a first-year university student from my church and I am the teacher-advisor for the Christian fellowship group at school. (Loyal Believer 25, Christian and Missionary Alliance)

I have now been involved in two churches which deliberately initiated a mentoring program for the church's youth group, where each young person who was interested was linked up with an older member of the congregation. (The young man I was linked with nearly 30 years ago is still a good friend of the family, and godfather to my now adult son.) More than one respondent requests that "mentors in their mid- to late- 20's and older mentors should be part of youth groups" and that churches "set up mentoring programs for people up to age 30."

In order for this to happen, of course, people need help in understanding the dynamics of mentoring. Preaching and study groups are two places where congregations can begin to learn about mentoring. Sometimes, pastors are worried that if they are involved in mentoring a small number of church members it can look like favouritism—and that is a real danger. However, relationships with the inner leadership team, whether it be the elders, small group leaders, or parish council, can easily have a mentoring dimension without it appearing to be (or indeed being) favouritism. It is one way to begin to develop a culture of mentoring.

Youthfulness

Another more controversial aspect of community that respondents look for is "a youthful church" (thirteen say this kind of thing). The following comments are typical:

> Traditional churches . . . are usually filled with older people I really don't have much in common with. (Loyal Believer 24, Anglican)

> [I hope to find] a church that I enjoy, with a young, excited congregation. (Absent Believer 32, United)

I find it striking that a word like "youthful" will often be paired with another word such as "vibrant," "stimulating," "encouraging," "relaxed," "friendly and welcoming," or even "spiritual." There is no logical reason, of course, why a church of seniors should not be like this. But my respondents seem to assume that only a church of young people can feel like this; or perhaps they have never found a church like this that wasn't a church of young people. However that may be, it is still true that it is not the average age of the congregation alone that is important, but the spirit of the congregation. Churches which sense they have lost that youthful spirit, regardless of their average age, should look into some of the many programs available today to help a church recover its vitality.[11]

Of course, there is the danger of a vicious circle when young people look for a church of young people. If they find no young people in a particular congregation, they won't go, and so it remains a church of older people. Some younger people and their families, of course, may feel called to stick with an older congregation, and hopefully begin a change.

---

11. One of the most popular and effective is Natural Church Development. NCD's approach and materials may be found on their website <www.ncdcanada. com>.

More often, however, churches which are ageing—of which there are many—cannot expect a young family to commit to their congregation if they are going to be the only one. Rather, a wise pastor will (perhaps sadly) refer them to a church where there are other families—even if it is a church of a different denomination.

But the chances are that a young family is more likely to stay if they detect that "youthful spirit"—stimulating, encouraging, friendly and even (ideally) intergenerational. And that is possible for many churches when they find ways to rediscover their spiritual vitality.

OPEN TO QUESTIONS

Young people are very insistent that their churches should be open to questions. Ten respondents explicitly make this point. "Allow us to have doubts and ask questions," says one. "We need to embrace questions and challenges," says another. Churches should be "open to discuss other beliefs and ways of life in a positive manner," says a third. They seem to have been in too many congregations where they felt that difficult questions were not allowed, and they are no longer prepared to put up with it. These comments are typical:

> My church does not openly tackle intellectual and relevant issues, such as pluralism, gender issues, and evangelism in a pluralistic society. (Loyal Believer 24, United)

> I was not allowed to ask rigorous questions in my Christian community about the world and God. (Loyal Believer 28, United to Quaker)

> I was raised in a church where no answers were given about why things were done as they were. You went to church on Sundays, but for what? Church was never really explained to me. (Absent Believer 22, Roman Catholic)

Perhaps the fullest, most thoughtful answer is the following:

I realized that I had never been encouraged or even allowed to ask questions—not the big ones. The "answers" [I was given were] things like "You just have to trust," or "You just don't have enough faith." These answers make you feel guilty for having questions and really inhibit you from growing. Perhaps it was just my church, but they seem to keep you from asking questions and just brainwash you, in a sense programming you with the right answers and not really encouraging you to grow and ask questions of your own. It was this realization that made me question my faith the most. Today I have a church that encourages growth—encourages me to seek out the answers to seek out God. (Loyal Believer 29, Baptist to Presbyterian)

We have seen how damaging to faith it is when this kind of openness is absent. One factor in a Former Believer's loss of faith was the conviction "that there are questions that can't be answered with pat quotes from the Bible." Others have moved outside mainstream Christian churches in order to be able to do that, one to the Quakers and another to the Unitarians:

Church was very unsatisfying for a very long time . . . It took a long time to find a place where I was accepted and encouraged to ask questions that many churches found threatening. (Loyal Believer 28, United to Quaker)

I am extremely happy to have found the Unitarian Church . . . I think that it is important to continue to question one's faith. I think that it is a difficult thing to do, and I think people should be able to discuss it freely and without fear. (Uncertain Believer 31, United to Unitarian)

Others, from a wide range of denominational backgrounds, when asked what they hope for in a church, speak of a need for:

[People] who are interested in exploring their own understanding of the "Christian experience" with an open and unassuming mind. (Absent Believer 30, Presbyterian)

Open ideas to people and society. (Absent Believer 25, United)

A setting that does not discourage doubt or independent thought
. . . I want to be engaged and encouraged to think for myself
about the idea being presented—to test how it compares with
my knowledge of God's character. (Loyal Believer 24, Anglican)

[People to be] open to discuss other beliefs and ways of life in a
positive manner. (Absent Believer 30, Christian Reformed)

Opportunity to discuss on an intellectual level my concerns
with traditional Christian ethos without pressure or ridicule.
(Absent Believer 25, United)

[A church] where people do not just accept what they are told at
face value. (Absent Believer 24, Baptist)

Real Christians talking about doubt, failure and not finding God
. . . Freedom to question. (Absent Believer 23, non-denominational)

[A church] willing to question and be open-minded; a place
where a diversity of people gather. (Absent Believer 23, United)

At least one person wants to clarify that this does not necessarily
imply any departure from traditional belief:

Room for discussion and differing opinions on sensitive issues,
although no room for bending God's word. (Absent Believer 38,
Baptist)

Once again, it seems a strange thing that churches following
someone who called himself "the truth"[12] have such a narrow view
of truth, and sometimes seem unwilling to consider how their
"truth" relates to life's difficult questions. One respondent believes
that "If truth is truth, it will out." Not all churches seem to share
that confidence.

The challenge is to be open to new ideas on the one hand, and
to be discerning about when to change and when not to change on

---

12. John 14:6

the other. If conservative churches are known for their inflexibility (and the number of comments suggest this is the case), the opposite tendency is also possible, that in liberal churches the baby gets thrown out with the bath water (and some will probably experience this, if they have not done so already). Having an open mind is good, but, as G. K.Chesterton said, "The object of opening the mind, as of opening the mouth, is to shut it again on something solid."[13]

SOCIAL CONCERN

Once upon a time, Christians made a distinction between evangelism (trying to save people's souls) and social concern (caring for their physical well-being). Evangelical Christians did the first and mainline Christians did the second. And neither had a very high opinion of the other.

That distinction means nothing to this generation, and they are especially impatient of churches who want only to do evangelism and are not interested in serving people in other ways. As they see it, the mix of word and action that Jesus and the early church modeled needs to work its way into the life of every church.[14] They are looking for:

> A different kind of church. One that is poor because of how it uses its money. One that is grassroots, has incredible integrity, is involved with the community, is being Jesus instead of (ironically) asking what He would do. (Absent Believer 27, Anglican)

Once again, these do not seem to be unreasonable demands of an institution that claims to be following in the footsteps of Jesus. Specifically, respondents ask for a church that is:

---

13. G. K.Chesterton, *Autobiography* (London: Hutchinson and Co., 1936; London: Hamish Hamilton, 1986), 223-224.

14. John Stott makes the same point in his book *Christian Mission in the Modern World* (Downers Grove: InterVarsity Press, 1975), especially chapter 1.

Practical. (Absent Believer 30, Anglican)

Exhibiting international concern. Involved with the wider community, not necessarily in an evangelistic way. (Absent Believer 26, non-denominational)

Interested in what Christianity has to say (and do) about issues of social justice and responsibility (Absent Believer 23, United)

Churches need to become more active in the world and actually seek to make a difference regarding the environment, world peace, poverty, abuse etc. (Loyal Believer 32, Anglican to Mennonite)

One writer asks for "Activities to go alongside the learning." (Absent Believer 24, Associated Gospel Church) Another sums up the need: "I heard about what Jesus did, tell what I can do." (Absent Believer 30, United)

A church that offers opportunities to serve overseas or among the poor in Canada will be welcome to Absent Believers. They are not looking for a "comfortable pew," but for opportunities to serve and grow. In one of his videos, Tony Campolo explains that one of the tasks young people need to undertake at their age is to discover that their lives can have meaning, and that what they do matters. Then he adds: "Young people want heroism—and churches offer them entertainment." Youth ministry that revolves around pizza and movie nights will only duplicate what people can easily get anywhere else. Churches that offer challenging opportunities to serve the world will help satisfy the yearning of young people to make a difference. They will also represent Jesus better.

THE STYLE AND CONTENT OF THE SERVICE

Music

As one would expect, there is a range of opinions on the topic of what church services should look like. One asks for "Good music (more Bach)" (Absent Believer 28, Catholic) whereas another confesses, "Singing upbeat songs would help my attendance." (Absent Believer, 30 United), whereas a third wants something in between:

> If I found a church that was in between the liturgy of Anglicanism and a simple "seeker" church—I loved the services at camp but can't find a church that is what I want. (Absent Believer 33, Anglican)

In the focus group, one woman suggested that the kind of music being offered was not as important as the fact that it was "tolerably well" done. In other words, people have preferences when it comes to style of worship, but it is not the only factor, nor the most important factor.

One of the other factors that a number of respondents mention is:

Preaching

A dozen respondents want to make a point about preaching. They ask for it to be strong and intellectually challenging, to deal well with the Bible, to address today's questions, and to have a practical edge. Here are some of their comments:

> I generally do not find the Sunday morning message typically delivers significant value. I find that many pastors seem to target a low common denominator for attendees. (Loyal Believer 37, Anglican to Christian and Missionary Alliance)

> Quite often teaching does not take into consideration anything contextual from the Bible and jumps around from text to text trying to prove the preacher's point beyond the shadow of a doubt. (Loyal Believer 24, Anglican)

Several use the term intellectual (for example, preaching should be "intellectually stimulating and challenging"); one says that preaching should be scholarly.

The same number of respondents want the preaching to connect with the hearers' lives. Respondents ask for such things as:

"Inspiring sermons that deal with recent issues" (Absent Believer 27, United); "Relate sermons to life's problems today" (Absent Believer 30, United); "Practical modern day advice" (Absent Believer 22, Anglican); and "Relevant sermons" (Absent Believer 23, Christian and Missionary Alliance).[15]

Someone looking for a church for the first time is likely to judge the church mainly by its Sunday service. But for someone who is already a Christian and is looking for a new church, they know there are other things that are also important. They are more likely to look for intangible things to do with the church's culture: we have highlighted the sense of community, a youthfulness of outlook, openness to questioning, and a strong social conscience.[16]

If they find those things present, they will be fairly tolerant of what happens on a Sunday morning. There are two things they ask of the Sunday service, however:

- for the music (of whatever kind) to be competently done, and
- for preaching which stretches the mind and heart.

And, of course, there are many churches which live up to these standards, and large numbers of Loyal and Returned Believers have gratefully found spiritual homes there.

TWO WARNINGS

There are two warnings for churches wanting to involve young Christians in their community:

---

15. Posterski and Barker found the same thing in their research: "Almost three-quarters of respondents said the quality of the preaching was a 'high priority.' Mainline and conservative respondents share exactly the same view." Posterski and Barker 186.

16. Peter Brierley has rightly suggested that an implied fifth factor is "the vision of the leader, without which the first four fail" (Personal correspondence with author).

Don't burn them out

If a church wants to win (or win back) young people, it can do all the right things and still lose members—if it demands too much of them. This is easy to do. As Posterski and Barker point out: "There is a tendency in organizational life to over-use the more talented and willing members."[17]

This has already happened to some of my respondents. They say things like this:

> If I think of the times when I was seriously involved in church as an adult, I left because the demands were too much. (Absent Believer 35, United to Presbyterian)

Others say they left because of:

> Burn out in Christian leadership. Did not attend a church regularly for 4-5 years. (Returned Believer 30, Baptist to Mennonite)

> Having done it all: too much involvement and being "over-churched." (Returned Believer 28, Baptist)

> Overload of Christians and Christian activities. I felt I had lost touch with the real world. (Returned Believer 24, Baptist to Anglican)

Three things are clear from the responses of Loyal and Returned Believers:

- they have discovered their limitations, sometimes the hard way;
- they may withdraw from leadership from time to time when they need it; and
- wise churches are understanding and give their leaders (especially with young families) a "sabbatical" as needed. [18]

---

17. Posterski and Barker, 59.

18. Posterski and Barker advise that "The effective church is one which

Listen to the comments:

> We are just figuring out where we can contribute in our new church. But wow, feeling the pressure to be involved, but with two small children and no Sunday school, not sure how to be helpful. (Returned Believer 36, Baptist)

> Due to some significant family needs we have stepped down for a season of focus on home and family. (Loyal Believer 35, none to Free Evangelical)

> I have been involved in Sunday school, youth work, preaching, drama, presentations, events, hospitality, 20-30s, administration etc. etc. I am now taking a needed break. (Loyal Believer 27, Anglican)

> My family and I belong to a small church. Many requests for taking on increased church responsibilities have been made of us. My wife started up a woman's Bible study group. I have a desire to do the same for the men yet, have made a conscious decision to hold off on that presently in order to keep a balance with present pursuits outside of church duties (professional and educational). (Loyal Believer 36, Presbyterian to Baptist)

> [I am doing] Too much at the moment. I am learning to say no and enjoy the ministries that I am good at, instead of feeling guilty and saying yes and then resenting having to help. (Loyal Believer 32, Christian Reformed)

It is very easy for a church to overburden young, enthusiastic members (especially those who have had training in leadership) with responsibilities. But the results are inevitable: burnout and dropping out. When that has happened, even when people return in the end (and not all of them will), they will be much more wary of taking on commitments the next time.[19] As one says:

. . . can anticipate possible burn-out before it happens" (Ibid., 59).

19. Returned Believers, as we have seen, are as active as Loyal Believers: but not many Returned Believers left because of burnout.

I am hesitant to commit whole heartedly to the ministry of our church as I know how all-consuming it can become. (Loyal Believer 25, United to Baptist)

There needs to be honest negotiation about how much people can take on, especially when they are thinking about entering (or re-entering) church life, and are keen to serve God in the church. On the one side, church leaders need to be pastorally sensitive, and not just think of the need to have every job filled. On the other side, young leaders need to be discerning about when to say yes. Otherwise, everybody suffers, in the short term and the long term.

Help people when they move

Churches can do more to help people when they move to a new city. This is when many people lose touch with church and, in some cases, with faith.[20] A church's care for its members does not end when they announce they are leaving for another place. One of the most valuable things a church can do is to recommend two or three churches in the area to which the member is moving. In some cases, it will also be appropriate (with permission, of course) to pass on the information to the leaders of the church in the new location.

Reginald Bibby suggests that denominational networks can be helpful in making these connections.[21] However, this may not be enough. There is simply too much evidence that people are willing to switch denomination in order to find a church they like. For example, if someone is leaving an evangelical Anglican church which has a large number of young families, the chances of them getting involved in a liberal Anglican church whose average age is over 60 in a new town is virtually nil. It is just not going to happen. They are far more likely to start going to a nearby Associated Gospel Church which is evangelical and family-oriented.

---

20. Bibby 1995, 78.
21. Ibid., 80–86.

If pastors are going to help members make the transition to a new town, therefore, they need to develop networks of churches outside their own denominations, and not only inside it. This can be done by building connections with interdenominational ministerial fellowships, or reading cross-denominational publications like the evangelical newspaper *ChristianWeek*. An internet search of church websites in the new area would also reveal something of the flavour of specific churches, and not just their denominational affiliation.

Of course, denominational contacts could still help. In an ideal world, for example, a Baptist pastor in city A could email a colleague in city B, describe a member who is moving to B, and the pastor in city B would say, "Hmm, to be honest I don't think our church would be a good fit, but there's a Free Methodist church closer to where these folks are moving. Let me give you the name and phone number of that pastor."

Is this kind of broadmindedness too much to ask? It depends which is more important to a church and its leaders: loyalty to the denomination or concern for the larger Kingdom? Trying to keep our members within the denominational fold or seeking whatever is for their spiritual good?[22]

CONCLUSION

The question "Where's a good church?" is really a Protestant kind of question. The Catholic or Anglican's first question would not be, "Where's a good church?" but "Where's the parish church?" and the question of whether it is "good" would hardly enter into it. The idea of the parish church is that it is simply the gathering of the Christians in a given neighbourhood. They are then a corporate witness in the area, not just on Sundays but through the week. In this kind of

---

22. Bibby believes he is "thinking idealistically" (85) by suggesting better intra-denominational tracking—in which case my proposal is even more hopelessly idealistic.

tradition, worshipping, working and living in the same neighbour-hood as fellow Christians may not always be easy, any more than living with one's family is always easy. Yet the discipline of having to hang in with the people God has put in my neighbourhood, rather than those I naturally like and drive across the city to be with, is a good one.

The question of finding a "good church," on the other hand, assumes that the individual Christian has good criteria and a moral right to pick and choose between churches. The church scene within half an hour's drive of my home becomes a smorgasbord where I can "taste and see" whether what is being offered is something that I am comfortable with, that suits my personal tastes and lifestyle, and that meets my felt needs. We look for "an exciting worship leader, good music, social action program, shared concerns, self-help recovery groups, religious education, even a large and convenient parking lot."[23] We get involved in what William Hendricks calls "the dance of the marketplace."[24]

Having said that, of course, our culture for the past three hundred years has reinforced the right of the individual to choose, and the fact that I have a car means I can drive as far as I like to attend a church of my choice. More than that, there may be good reasons why my local parish church is not one that I want to be involved in, and I may find myself grateful for the fact that there are other choices available.

The fact is that these days most people will choose whether to go to church and where to go to church. When they do, they may simply go to their local church because there is good sense in doing so. But they are more likely to shop around (a significant phrase) for

---

23. Roof and Johnson, in Roozen and Hadaway, 306–307.
24. William D. Hendricks, *Exit Interviews* (Chicago: Moody Press, 1993), 294–295.

the right church for them. Which means (to continue the metaphor) that it is a buyer's market, as far as churches are concerned. [25]

Yet I am struck again by the fact that what respondents to this survey are looking for seems quite reasonable:

- that a group of followers of Jesus should cultivate a warm and open community
- that they should consider issues of truth
- that they should be active in service, and
- that worship (whatever form it takes) should be done with excellence and should include thoughtful preaching.

Surely these are criteria that are basic for any church. Indeed, if these things are not important to a congregation, maybe it is time to stop and think: Who are we as a community? What exactly are our values? How can we begin to make these things more central to our identity as a community of followers of Jesus?

---

25. For those who attended Pioneer Camp, there is an alumni list to which former campers can subscribe. One potential use of such a list is to find out what churches people are involved in and where.

10

REFLECTIONS ON
THE JOURNEY

An Open Letter

Dear Reader:

I do not know who you are. After all, various people might be reading this book. Perhaps you were one of the people who responded to the study. Maybe you recognized your own words in what you have read. Perhaps you were invited to respond but chose not to, and you are simply curious to measure your own experience against that of others. Or maybe you have been interested to know what shapes the spiritual journey of young people these days. I imagine some of you are parents or grandparents or youth pastors with a heart concern for very specific young people.

Whoever you are, I want to end on a more personal note than was possible in the rest of the book. Hence the idea of an "open letter" to you.

Part of the initial impetus for this study was a personal one. I wanted to know what had happened to all those people that I and many other leaders had given a piece of our lives to. It is tempting to use financial imagery: did we make a wise investment? Has there been a good return? Was it profitable? Did the dividends justify the outlay? While I do not think this kind of imagery is always helpful, the answer in part is clearly, Yes: the goal of the leadership program was to help equip Christian leaders for the future, and many have clearly become Christian leaders—in churches, in business, in the arts, at home, and in schools. Certainly there have been many other influences which have contributed to that, but the leadership program at Pioneer has been one of those, however small in proportion to the rest of life.

And what about those who have given up on Christian faith— obviously many more than the fourteen who took the time to tell me about it? Was that an investment that failed? I would have to say, No. Naturally, I am saddened by some of the stories, sometimes by the choices people have made, more often by the church's failure and even abuse of young people. Yet love, if it is real love, is prepared to give, whatever the results, even if there are none. Love is not an "investment" which anticipates certain "dividends": it is a gift, with no strings attached. This is how God's love is, after all: God hopes for a response, but God's love is a gift. So I have come to the conviction that it was an undiluted good for us to be able to give time and love, instruction and a listening ear to those young people— whatever became of them later.

Having said that, the personal dimension of this study has not gone away. Indeed, it has taken on a new depth. As I have read over what people have said about why they stayed Christians, or moved away, or kept faith but gave up on church, I find myself asking: So why am *I* still a Christian? I made the transition from church participant to committed follower of Jesus when I was sixteen, the same age as the respondents were when we first met. For me, that is over forty years ago.

Why do I keep going? Has it been all sweetness and light? Of course not. Have there been no doubts? No times of difficulty? Yes, of course. I have known long periods of doubt and spiritual darkness, the worst lasting several years. I have had prayers go unanswered which were desperately urgent. Indeed, on some days I can see quite clearly how this whole world could be a random product of natural causes, a fluke of the universe, and all our talk about God mere nonsense. Some days I am tempted by the idea of Deism—the theory that there is a Creator, but that this God has a hands-off approach to the day-to-day running of the world. Certainly the world looks that way quite frequently: it would neatly explain why prayers are so seldom answered. And some days I think death really is the end, and that the rest is just so much wishful thinking.

There is more. I have been embarrassed by the failure of Christ's followers, now and through history, to live up to his name—and even more by my own failure to do so. Some days I see so little of Jesus in the church or in my life that I think it would be easier just to be a nice pagan (and there are many of them) and take a long break from all the complexities and nonsense of church life.

So why am I still a Christian? Why do I hang in with faith and (even stranger) with church? Here's what I have come up with. Maybe it will be helpful if you are asking yourself the same question.

Let me summarise it, and then unpack it a little: I am still a Christian because I believe God is calling human beings to follow Jesus, so that the world may be restored to the way the Creator longs for it to be. I am a Christian because I want to respond to that call and to play my part in the restoration project.

Behind this conviction lies the three-fold Christian understanding of life, the Christian worldview if you like: that God made this world, and made it good; that something has gone horribly wrong in the world, largely because human beings have failed to follow the Creator's norms for living; and, thirdly, that God is seeking to put things to rights through Jesus, his life and teaching, his death and resurrection.

In particular, God is wanting to bring into being a community following Jesus which will be the centerpiece of the project, and to work alongside him to bring it about. This will be a community where people learn what human relationships should be like and what it means to live as a human being in God's world.

This is why I hang in with the church. In spite of its numerous failings (some of which I have contributed to), the church is at its heart a simple concept: a community of people coming together from all walks of life with the simple goal of learning to love God and love their neighbour—the two Great Commandments. That seems to me an ideal that is breathtakingly simple (1. get together, 2. love God, 3. love one another) and at the same time absolutely crazy (it's hard enough to get on with our family sometimes—and you want us to love all these strangers?). Who would ever think such a thing was a good idea? Well, God our Creator, that's who.

We shouldn't be surprised by the times when the church goes wrong. After all, churches are full of sinful, self-centred, hurting, confused people—and, when we attend, we just add to their number. (Not that church is unique in this respect: that's just how the human race is.) It is when we forget that this is the case that we get into trouble.

At least two New Testament images of church remind us of what the church is: it is a hospital ("Those who are well have no need of a physician but those who are sick"[1]) and it is like a school ("You call me Teacher and Lord—and you are right for that is what I am"[2]) Both are reminders that people in church are works-in-progress, and thus cause for great humility. If the church is a spiritual hospital, for instance, we know that special care is needed as patients care for one another under the direction of the Doctor. Nobody expects full health in anybody else, and even small improvements are cause for celebration. And if church is a school for learning God's ways from Jesus the Teacher, nobody has yet graduated, everybody is

---

1. Mark 2:17
2. John 13:13

struggling to learn particular lessons, and some successes and many failures are to be expected.

But this calling is a tough one. We don't like to be reminded that we are patients in need of healing; we don't enjoy being in a context where we have to work at being students once again. It is far easier to get involved in the secondary things of church life, whether leadership or liturgy, finance or politics. Don't get me wrong: these are important too. Yet they are only important as they help us love God and love our neighbour. Too often our calling to follow Jesus degenerates into a concern for religion. Secondary things take centre-stage.

But there are times when the church gets it right. The Doctor's therapy program is beginning to produce health, the students are learning some of the Teacher's key lessons. Then the results can be impressive. A leader in my own church died not long ago after eight weeks of terminal illness. The church did a magnificent job of caring for him and his family through that time, and continues to do so. The neighbours could hardly believe their eyes at the stream of people coming and going to do whatever needed to be done—to pray, to care, and just to be present. I was reminded of the words of one elderly lady: "If you join this church, you will never have to carry a burden alone again."

Then there are also times when the church is faithful to its calling on a larger scale. In the spring of 2004, veteran CBC reporter Brian Stewart spoke at the convocation of Knox College in Toronto, and talked openly about how the example of Christians around the world had driven him back to his childhood faith. He said things like this:

> I've found there is no movement, or force, closer to the raw
> truth of war, famines, crises, and the vast human predicament,
> than organized Christianity in action. And there is no alliance
> more determined and dogged in action than church workers,
> ordained and lay members, when mobilized for a common good.
> It is these Christians who are right "On the Front Lines" of
> committed humanity today and when I want to find that front, I

follow their trail . . . I have never been able to reach these front lines without finding Christian volunteers already in the thick of it, mobilizing congregations that care, and being a faithful witness to truth, the primary light in the darkness and so often, the only light . . . Let me repeat, I've never reached a war zone, or famine group or crisis anywhere where some Church organization was not there long before me . . . sturdy, remarkable souls usually too kind to ask, "What took you so long?"[3]

Such stories give me heart. This *does* work, or at least it *can* work. The struggles, the folly, the brokenness—all these bearable as long as there are glimpses of the reality that Jesus really is at work in this church that bears his name, and that he is doing something new and beautiful.

Thus when I think about why I am still a Christian involved in church, it is because I believe God is at work in the world, and that somehow God's work is in a unique way channeled through Jesus Christ—his life, death and resurrection, his Spirit at work in the world—and through the people who gather to worship him and learn from him. I want to be there, on the one hand trying to help the church be that vehicle of God's love and truth and joy to the world, and on the other hand learning from Jesus and his church what my role is in the project.

And as I do that, I try to keep in mind that church is not a religious game. It is first and last about the Creator's global restoration project. In my humble opinion, there is no more worthwhile adventure for human beings to give their lives to.

Sincerely,
John Bowen

3. The full text of Brian Stewart's speech can be read at: http://www.utoronto.ca/knox/dconadd04.htm

LaVergne, TN USA
04 October 2010
199527LV00003BA/32/P

9 781573 834315